OSCAR I AM!

Patriots Point Institute of History, Science & Technology
Mt. Pleasant, SC

PATRIOTS POINT
★ HOME OF THE USS YORKTOWN ★

Text by Hannah Giddens
Oscar and Friends created by Keith Grybowski
Cover design by Jim Vickers and Cindy Lee
Illustrations & cover art by Hannah Giddens
Proofreading and technical aid by Alicia Raimann

ISBN 978-0-985920432
Manufactured in the United States

TABLE OF CONTENTS

Note to Teachers and Parents

This book illustrates fifth grade South Carolina science standards within the context of a story.

Oscar, Hank and Hannah make up a water molecule, and together they travel through a variety of South Carolina's ecosystems - literally bringing science standards to life. Readers will discover different aspects of physical, earth and life science as they follow this traveling trio across an ocean and down watersheds.

You will notice that, not only will this literary adventure reinforce fifth grade concepts, but review standards from lower grades and hit on ideas that will be soon to come in their young scientific careers.

Each chapter comes with illustrations, vocabulary, fun facts and critical thinking questions. At the end of the book are chapter extensions to further enrich the student's experience. Extensions include informational text, math concepts, experiments and crafts. Please note that the reading level for each main chapter on the Flesch-Kincaid scale is listed in italicized parentheses in the table of contents. Thought was taken into providing a variety of reading level opportunities.

To continue the adventure, we invite you to take advantage of the many resources supporting this book, including those found on our website www.Patriotspoint.org. For the ultimate educational experience, please visit us aboard the aircraft carrier USS *Yorktown*, in Mt. Pleasant, South Carolina.

Happy reading from Oscar and friends!

Introduction – The Briefing

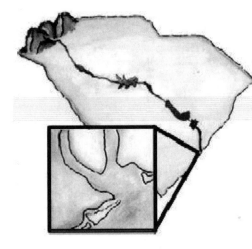

Hey there, kids!

You're invited to embark on a scientific adventure with the most important molecule to life on our planet: water.

Oscar, Hank and Hannah will guide you through South Carolina's ecosystems as they take part in the water cycle. Follow this traveling trio across an ocean and down watersheds. Your journey will include stops in a variety of ecosystems. As a budding scientist, at each stop you are invited to answer the critical thinking questions at the end of each chapter.

To help you on your journey, you'll find at the end of each chapter a travel guide of fun facts, concepts, vocabulary words, and case studies for more in-depth discussions. Refer to them any time you have questions about a word you encounter or a process discussed.

Remember to have fun, experience the wonders, and enjoy the trip!

Chapter 1

Meet

Oscar,

Hank

and

Hannah

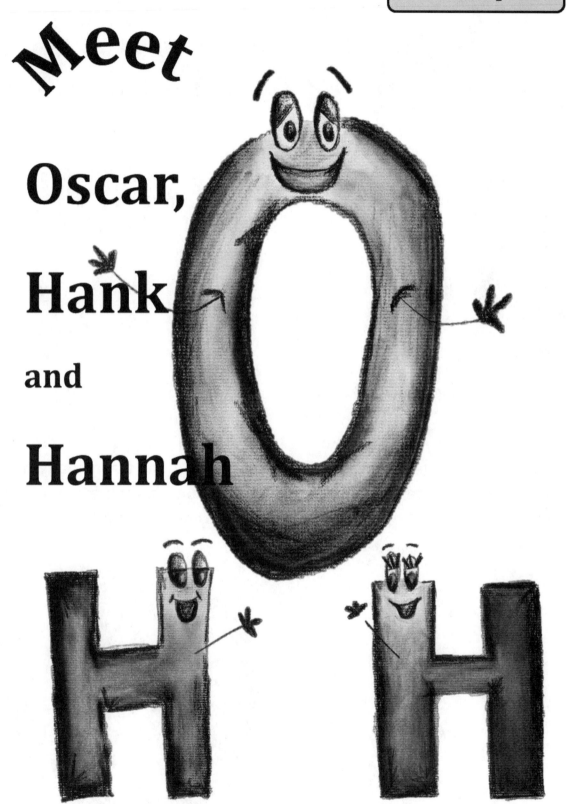

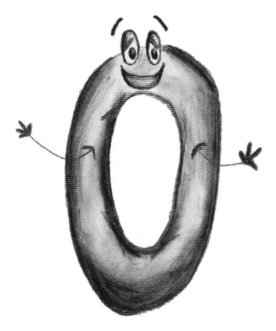

Hey everyone! My name is Oscar. I am an **oxygen** atom. I have been around for a long time, and I have a story to share. My friends Hank and Hannah have been begging me to write it down. I have decided to give it a try, so I will start from the very beginning.

I have been on planet Earth for many years. For most of those years I have been hanging out with Hank and Hannah as a water **molecule**. What is a molecule, you ask? In case you didn't know, **matter** is made up of tiny particles. These particles are too small to see. These particles are called **atoms**. I am an oxygen atom. (Gee whiz, I hope you didn't forget that already!) Hank and Hannah are **hydrogen** atoms. When one oxygen atom joins two hydrogen atoms, a water molecule is formed. I have spent a lot of time as a water molecule. It is pretty awesome.

A Watery World...

Water is really neat. Water is also very important. It can be a **solid**, **liquid** or **gas**. As a solid, water is called ice. As a gas, water is called water vapor. Did you know about 70% of Earth's surface is covered in water? Another water fact is that cells are made of 70-95% water. Cells are the smallest unit of life. If there was no water there would be no life! Even the human body is about 60% water! In fact, I have spent time in organs, muscles, bones and blood! Many reactions required for plants and animals to survive need water. This means that you would not be alive without Hank, Hannah and me as water.

Matter on Earth is not created and not destroyed. Matter on Earth is recycled. Water on Earth has been in oceans, storms and glaciers. The water that comes out of your faucet has been drunk from dinosaurs to you!

It is important to tell water's story as more and more people inhabit the planet we share. Hank, Hannah and I agree that water needs to be appreciated, respected and protected. So are you ready for a wild ride? Here we go...

- **atom** - the building block of matter

- **element** - a substance that cannot be broken down chemically, it is pure and made up of all of the same kinds of atoms

- **hydrogen** - the smallest, lightest **element** that helps make up water and sugars

- **mass** - the amount of material in matter

- **matter** - anything that takes up space and has **mass**

- **molecule** - a combination of two or more atoms

- **oxygen** - an **element** necessary for the survival of most life on earth; it is one of the two elements that make up water and as a gas it is in the air we breathe

- (see below for solid, liquid and gas)

Did you know?

- In a **solid**, molecules are tightly packed and have just enough room to vibrate. In a **liquid**, molecules can move about, taking the shape of their container. Because of gravity, the surface of a liquid is flat. In a **gas**, molecules move rapidly and can have great distances between them.

- In 1789, Antoine Lavoisier described The Law of Conservation of Mass. It says that all of the atoms making up matter on Earth are recycled. They may go through physical and even chemical changes forming new molecules, but an oxygen atom has always been an oxygen atom and it always will be.

1. Can you challenge yourself to recognize all of the objects and matter around you as atoms and molecules? Are they tightly packed? Are they contained but still flowing and moving fluidly, or are they bouncing around the room? Write about one object below.

2. If all of the matter on our planet is recycled, then is water a limited resource? Depending on your answer, how could water as a limiting factor affect our human population on Earth?

Chapter 2

Forming the STORM!

This story begins off of the coast of Africa in the sky over the Atlantic Ocean, close to the equator. A warm tropical breeze was blowing. The water sparkled. The sun made the silver fish swimming below shine and glimmer. The sky was clear and sunny. There were no clouds. Once in a while sea birds flapped past. They would rest their wings and glide on gusts of wind. Even though the weather was perfect, we couldn't get rid of the feeling that something wasn't right.

Hank, Hannah and I had been blowing around for weeks as water vapor. We hovered just above the ocean. When we are water vapor, we are a gas. As a gas, most people don't see us because we are transparent. People really only see us when we have **condensed** from a gas to a liquid like when we fog up a bathroom mirror after a hot shower.

So there we were. Enjoying the sun and floating on a breeze. Hank was saying how he could really take a nap. Before he could finish his sentence a gust of wind began to take us higher and higher.

The higher we climbed, the colder the air became. I noticed other water molecules around us also traveling higher. Suddenly out of nowhere - SMACK! SMACK!

"Eeeeeooooowwwwww!" Hannah screamed.

Whack! Something hit me hard. "What is going on here?" I shouted.

Then I realized what was going on. Did you know it isn't all gas up in the atmosphere? Bits of solids, like tiny pieces of dirt and dust, and liquids can hang out in the sky too. When water vapor slams into these bits of solids, well, look at what happens next.

We kept climbing. We were getting thumped and bumped. The air was getting colder. Hannah rolled her eyes and said, "Here we go again, you two. Just when I thought being a gas was great, it looks like we are going to be a liquid again."

 It was true. Going through these physical changes was a drag. And then IT HAPPENED. BAM! The air was cool enough. We hit another dust particle and CONDENSED! We noticed water vapor all around us changing from a gas to a liquid. And boy, it was windy.

We shouted hello to some water molecules that were pushed into us with all of the wind. They waved back looking scared. Soon our group was large enough and had enough **mass** to be called a cloud droplet.

Suddenly, Hannah pointed. Her eyes were wide and her face crinkled up and cringed. She yelled, "Brace for impact!"

We were struck by a larger droplet. It was like it completely sucked us up! I looked around and everyone seemed tired, but was smiling. We even had new friends joining us. From a distance we noticed sunlight reflecting off of the many cloud droplets. We looked like a beautiful feather.

Hank told Hannah he thought we were becoming a **cumulonimbus cloud**. He was right. We were steadily rising higher. Our cloud was growing quickly. Soon we were over the ocean as a tall, stormy cloud. We looked more like lumpy mashed potatoes now instead of a feather.

I admit I was getting excited. I was hoping we would become a **hurricane**. I was also hoping that it would take us to the East Coast of the United States. As if Hank and Hannah read my mind, they both exclaimed together, "We've never been to the East Coast before!"

A **hurricane** is an organized group of rotating clouds & thunderstorms with wind speeds of at least 74 miles per hour.

So we were gusting and swirling and hoping our baby storm would grow and rain us down somewhere new.

Vocabulary

- **condense** – to make denser, in this case – the process of condensation where a gas physically changes into a liquid

- **cumulonimbus cloud** – thunderstorm clouds that grow in height

- **mass** – the amount of material in matter

- Liquids and gases will take the shape of the container they are in. Gas molecules will spread out within the container. If there is no container, gas molecules will disperse into their surroundings.

- Cloud droplets often form on particles of dust that are transported by wind in the atmosphere. Water vapor must be able to condense onto some sort of particle. We call those particles cloud condensation nuclei.

- Warm air holds more water vapor than cold air. As temperatures drop in the atmosphere, clouds can form.

- Cloud droplets can collide with one another. They coalesce. That means they stick together and become one.

- Cyclones and hurricanes are both big rotating storms with thunderstorms and high winds. The difference in the name is simply due to the location! Hurricanes occur in the Atlantic and Northeastern part of the Pacific and cyclones occur in the South Pacific and Indian Ocean.

Points to Ponder

1. How might a hurricane affect the area you live in? Do you have a natural disaster plan that you discuss with your family or school?

2. What other natural processes can you think of that might affect the place where you live in both constructive and destructive ways?

Chapter 3

To the Mountains I Shall Go, to Erode!

(Crash Landing on Table Rock)

We had now been spinning as part of a huge hurricane for almost one week. We watched cloud droplets all around us become larger and heavier.

Hank looked tired. He said to me, "Oscar, I think we might make it to the East Coast soon. All of the droplets around us are smashing into each other and growing. This morning we even collided with another one. We have so much mass now that soon we will be a rain droplet! Other parts of this storm have already been raining down."

Oxygens and hydrogens around us nodded their heads and agreed.

It was dark when our hurricane made landfall on the coast of South Carolina. We couldn't see a thing. It was hot. The air was sticky. Rain drops below and next to us started to fall. The **force** of **gravity** pulled them towards the land under us.

Our droplet hung in there, though. It felt like a while. After several hours it was bound to happen. Hannah pointed out that we felt very heavy. As soon as we were joined by another droplet it was like we had just started on a rollercoaster- straight down!

Hank was excited and yelled, "This is it! Hang on folks!"

We were falling and falling and falling.

Larger drops zoomed past us as we all held on tightly.

"I wish we could go faster!" I screamed.

Hannah did not like this at all. She shrieked. "No, no no! Slow down! Help!"

I raised my voice above the shouting, "You know what Hannah? After all of these years I would think you would start to enjoy this! I mean, it isn't like anything BAD is going to happen!"

As soon as I said that though, I regretted it. Why? Well, there happened to be what looked like an itty bitty mountain becoming larger and larger as we rushed towards it.

"We are falling towards that big green blob!" Hannah exclaimed.

"Green? That looks blue!" Hank argued.

"You two are nuts! I don't think the color of the blob matters!" I said.

The outlines of the tree tops and massive rocky faces were now easy to see. Oh yes, I thought. Nothing *bad* is happening. This is HORRIBLE!

Despite the scary situation, we were amazed. The storm had made its way past the coast and to the mountain region of South Carolina. All along the way the storm rained drops of water molecules it had picked up from the atmosphere over the ocean. Now that the storm was over land, it did not have a fresh supply of water molecules. The storm was weakening.

But let me get back to us rushing towards the ground. There we were, rushing towards the ground. What happened next reminds me of a bug on a windshield. We slammed into a rock face with a GREAT... BIG... SPLAT.

Rain drops splashed around us. They were rushing down the steep, almost vertical, face. We were swept downward and traveled together as a giant sheet of water. We were moving so quickly I almost didn't notice the new face that was now with us. The force of us smashing into the rock broke off a teensy weensy piece. That piece, turns out, was quite a character.

"I LOVE THIS!" shouted the teensy weensy piece of rock. "My name is Gus! I have been a part of that rock for ages! For thousands of years you water molecules have been splashing me in the face! I am a type of rock called granite. **Granite** is tough and strong and doesn't break apart, or **erode**, very easily. I have watched other mountain peaks **weather** and erode. My rock has held out longer than the others." Gus paused and turned to me. "By the way, where are you guys going?"

"Oh, just going with the flow," I answered. Gee whiz. That Gus liked to talk.

Gus talked. And he talked. And he talked some more. He told us about his life on **Table Rock**. As he talked we traveled from the rock face to more gentle hills. Gus kept talking to Hank and Hannah as he bounced around, sometimes banging into leaves, twigs and other rocks. Once and awhile he would knock into the rich soil. Bits of sand and clay were now carried along with our quickly moving group. I was starting to think this Gus was clumsy.

A voice in the rushing water called out of nowhere all of a sudden, "Hey y'all! My name is Sammy! I am a grain of sediment!"

I got a closer look as the water pushed him closer. What is sediment, I wondered. As if Sammy read my mind he explained himself.

"**Sediment** are particles like bits of rock or soil that have been eroded. These particles already have been and will one day be **deposited**. Oh boy, I can't wait to be deposited somewhere new! Don't worry you guys, I will explain that some other time," Sammy said.

"Well, Sammy, I am Oscar. These are my friends Hank and Hannah and our new friend Gus."

"Hi Sammy, sorry I disturbed you," apologized Gus.

"Oh, that is ok. I have been traveling down these mountains all summer. Every time a storm comes along I just roll with the water as it rains down and travels over land. These last two years my family and I were hanging onto the root of a blueberry bush. A white-tailed deer and her fawn came over and ate the bush into pieces! I thought they would never stop eating! The small bush did not recover. It did not have leaves to collect energy from the sun. With no energy from the sun the blueberry bush could not

photosynthesize. It slowly died. One night it was washed away with heavy rain. With no roots to keep the dirt in place, we washed away too."

"How horrible," Hannah cried.

Hank agreed, "That sounds like no fun at all!"

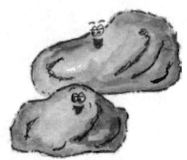

Sammy continued talking and added, "Y'all must have been part of a very big storm! This is a lot of water. I bet we will run into some sort of creek. That is what usually happens up here in the **Blue Ridge Region** as water drains from high places to lower places."

And that is when I decided two things. Gus and Sammy could chat on and on. When they did chatter they shared some helpful information.

Vocabulary

- **Blue Ridge Region** - this region in South Carolina containing the Blue Ridge Mountains covers about 2% of South Carolina and is located in the northwestern corner; the Blue Ridge Mountains are a part of the Appalachian mountain chain

- **deposit** - to settle, in this case referring to the geological process of deposition; **deposition**- the process in which sediment (Chapter 3) settles out of the water column the moment it stops moving

- **erosion** - the removal and transport of soil and rocks by water, wind, or ice

- **granite** - an igneous (volcanic) rock that is very hard to erode; granite is often used as building material and also makes up the Earth's continental crust (the outermost layer of Earth that makes up our continents)

- **gravity** - a force (a push or pull on an object because of its interaction with another object) in which one body (like a moon or planet) attracts other bodies towards them

- **photosynthesis** - a biochemical (see chapter 1) process in which light energy is used along with carbon dioxide (a gas) and water to produce sugar; photosynthesize is the act of going through photosynthesis

- **sediment** - particles (rock fragments, soil) that have been eroded and are or will be deposited

- **Table Rock** is a **monadnock** - a large hill or rock that stands alone because the surrounding landforms have eroded away; they are made of hard erosion resistant rock, which is why they are "alone"

- **weathering** - the wearing down of a rock or landform in place

Did you know?

- Hurricanes can grow and maintain their strength with a supply of warm ocean water. As hurricanes are traveling, they are raining. Without a fresh supply of water vapor in the atmosphere to replenish the rain clouds, the hurricane will weaken.

- Hurricanes typically weaken once they hit land for two reasons. One, their water supply is cut off. Two, the frictional force of the hurricane passing over the land can slow down the rotation of the storm.

- Frictional force is a force applied by an object onto another object that is moving or trying to move over it.

Points to Ponder

1. How many forces can you identify in this chapter? What objects or characters are involved? Can you describe the interactions between these objects?

2. A plant and its roots are very important to stabilizing soil and preventing erosion as well as helping to build up soil in a particular location (you will learn more about that process in chapter 4). What might be the impact on a hillside if trees are removed? What about if dune plants are removed from sand dunes on the beach?

Where are Oscar & his friends now?

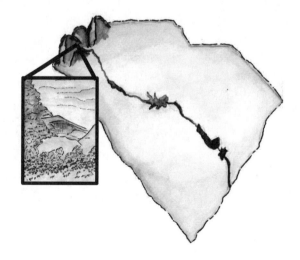

Streams, Rivers, Lakes – Oh My!
From the Mountains to the Saluda

Sunlight shone through the pines and mountain laurel. It dappled the ground we traveled over. It was not long before all of us spilled into a rapidly moving creek. The water we joined was clear, cool, and full of oxygen. The bottom was covered with smooth stones. The stones were different colors of white, gray and brown.

Suddenly a winged insect landed on the water's surface right next to us.

"AAAAH!" I yelped.

"Sorry to scare you," said the insect. "I just wanted to tell you new folks that while it is very pretty here, you need to be careful! As you head **downstream** there are **predators** hiding in the shadows!" And then, she flew off.

I wondered what she was talking about. No sooner did she leave than I saw a mouth. It was closing. It was opening. It was closing again. It was right in front of us.

We were headed straight for it!

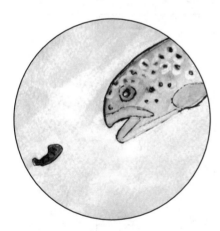

As we got closer I could see it was some sort of fish. It burst forward. It grabbed a **nymph** caught in the current next to us. With a gulp the nymph was gone. The fish turned to us with a toothy grin as we floated past.

"Don't worry," he said. "I really like to eat insects. I don't like to consume sediment and their liquid friends. And while we are on the topic of sediment, please try to keep it out of my stream!"

We were drifting and it was getting harder to hear him. I was able to hear him yell, "I am Buster, a brook trout!"

This was another close call. Thank goodness he was friendly! It must be a southern East Coast thing. This trip was filled with surprises.

We traveled on this way, five friends soaking in the sights and enjoying the day. We noticed the creek widening. We were entering a larger body of water. Another brook trout we passed told us we were entering the Oolenoy River. "Maybe you all will make it to the ocean one day! You are on the right path," the trout told us.

We all looked at each other in amazement.

"That would be AWESOME!" Gus exclaimed. "As long as I can remember I have been a part of the Earth's **mantle** and also the Earth's **crust**! The ocean would be great!"

We continued downstream. Day turned into night. Night turned into day. The landscape around us changed. What was mountain forest became farms and fields lining the riverbank. Rugged mountain land changed to gentle hills and valleys. The river had changed, too. Somewhere during the night it had joined a much wider body of water. It was now traveling slower and we were traveling slower with it. It was murky.

I noticed Gus was lagging behind. He was also starting to sink.

"Hey there Gus, what is going on? Are you feeling ok?" I asked.

"I feel fine. It is like the water isn't moving fast enough to carry me anymore. Maybe I am too heavy?" said Gus.

At that time a large stone beneath us spoke up. "That's correct. Sediment can be eroded and transported or deposited. It all depends on the movement of the water and the size of the sediment." The stone looked at Gus. "You are too heavy for the river traveling at this **speed**. It can't take you any farther. Look around you. It is only the smaller particles that are being held by the water here. But there are worse places. Personally I think this is a nice neighborhood."

Hannah, Hank and I signaled to Sammy for help grabbing Gus. Gus stopped us.

"It is ok you all. This is a nice river. I think I would like to live here for a bit. Do me a favor though, enjoy the ocean for me! Stay safe! I hope you all make it!"

We all waved farewell as Gus settled on the bottom of the Saluda River, where it joins Lake Greenwood. It took us all day to move through Lake Greenwood as we continued to move downstream with the Saluda. Where we were going and what we would see next we did not know. Excitement filled us as we thought about the possibilities.

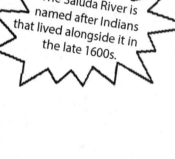

The Saluda River is named after Indians that lived alongside it in the late 1600s.

Vocabulary

- **crust**- the outermost layer of the Earth; it is thin and solid and can be divided into oceanic and continental crust

- **downstream** – going or sitting in the direction of the current in a body of water

- **mantle**- the dense, very hot, and mostly solid middle layers of the Earth

- **nymph**- the larvae of some invertebrates, typically insects

- **predator**- a consumer that kills other animals for food

- **speed** – is the distance an object travels over time

Did you know?

- When we think of solutions, we typically think of a solid dissolving in a liquid; however, gases can dissolve in liquids, also! Dissolved oxygen gas in water is how aquatic organisms (like fish) breathe.

- Temperature and stirring, or natural disturbances like waves and ripples, can affect the rate of dissolving. A mountain stream is oxygen rich, because colder water holds more oxygen gas than warm water and quickly moving shallow water over stones helps not only to "stir" the oxygen gas, but capture oxygen gas from the atmosphere (this will be introduced in Chapter 5).

- Brook trout can only survive in very clear, unpolluted (see pollutant in Chapter 5 vocabulary) streams. Because they require such pristine habitats, they are good indicators of the overall health of a mountain stream ecosystem.

- Granite is an igneous (volcanic) rock formed from cooling magma. Magma is hot, melted rock and is formed in the Earth's mantle.

Points to Ponder

- Brook trout, the only trout native to South Carolina, are very sensitive to sedimentation (the addition of sediment to a body of water). Looking back on what you have read so far, how might deforestation affect the brook trout?

- The flowing water Gus and his friends first traveled in was moving fast, and the force of the water on Gus was able to transport Gus downstream. As the river slows down, Gus is deposited on the bottom. What forces can you think of that slow Gus down and eventually cause him to stop moving with the river?

Where are Oscar & his friends now?

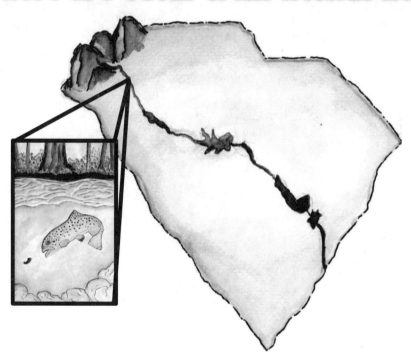

Chapter 5

History, Humans and the Dams

Journey to Dreher Shoals Dam

Once again, the moon rose as the night closed in. Crickets and frogs were making a racket. The night sky reflected off of the water like a mirror. We forgot to remain alert as we were lulled to sleep.

In the distance a boat motor cranked. It jarred us awake. I shook my head and blinked my eyes trying to dust the sleep off.

"Hey sleepy heads. Wake up. We are lost. Now we will never make it to the ocean!" Hannah complained.

"Good morning to you, too," said a groggy Sammy.

"There is no need to get worked up", said Hank with a yawn. "Everything is going to be fine."

"Well I don't think so," said Hannah snottily. "We are barely moving. We are far from any river bank. And look, this body is so large that if I didn't know any better I would think we already made it to the ocean! But I happen to know this is **fresh water**, not **salt water**."

We bickered. We didn't notice shadows slowly getting closer. The shadows were long and lean. They were silent. They crept in closer with a flick of their fins.

"Do you feel like we are being watched?" Sammy asked.

"Yes, I do," I said uneasily.

Hank and Hannah started looking around us. We were nervous. The shadows had us surrounded. The largest member of the group swam over and

I had a sinking feeling. This could not be good. This was one of the strangest fish I had ever seen. It reminded me of the times of dinosaurs, prehistoric times. It had large scales and a long thin jaw like an alligator.

"Hi everyone," said the fish. "I am Gary the Garfish. Sorry if we spooked you. We run a business. It is our job to make sure all of the tourists we get in these parts are following all of the rules and don't get lost."

"This is perfect!" I said. "We are trying to reach the Atlantic Ocean and visit the coast for a little while. Can you help us?"

"Absolutely we can," said Gary holding out his **pectoral fin**. "Welcome to Lake Murray. Please follow us."

It turned out that Gary and his Gar friends were very friendly and fun to be around. They knew all sorts of things about the area. They pointed out the sites and shared information. Lake Murray is a man-made lake in the **piedmont region** of South Carolina. The land was flooded in the 1930s to form a **reservoir** for a **hydroelectric dam**.

Gary was explaining many things. I could not help but still have a lot of questions. What was a reservoir? What was a hydroelectric dam? Gary promised me we would all understand once we reached the dam.

"For now though, there is much more to tell. Please pay attention," asked Gary. "The Lake Murray **ecosystem** is special and important. All ecosystems are made of living and nonliving things. We describe them as **biotic** and **abiotic**. These biotic and abiotic parts interact. The water (like you, Hank and Hannah), the sediment like Sammy brought here by the Saluda, and all of the plants and animals are connected. The number one way the living parts are connected is through food. **Producers** use energy from the sun to make food. We call that process photosynthesis."

"Like the blueberry bush Gus told us about!" exclaimed Hannah.

"That is right. Producers produce energy from the sun and **herbivores** eat the producers," said Gary.

"Like the deer in Gus's story!" nodded Hank.

"That is right again," continued Gary. "**Carnivores** prey on herbivores. There is more to the story, but we will leave it at that for now. What I really want to talk about are the humans."

"Ooohhhh,"said our group of friends in unison.

"I know a little about humans", offered Sammy. "They can be good and bad. I just think they need to learn about what is going on in the world around them."

"We agree", said Gary. All of the gars bobbed in agreement. "Our lake wouldn't be here without the humans. The humans need to follow the rules, though. Look over here." Gary nodded in the direction of a thick tangle of weeds. The weeds reached from the bottom all the way to the surface. "These plants were most likely released into this lake by accident. Now they are taking over. They compete with the **native** plants for space and sunlight. They use a lot of important oxygen, too."

"Hey, that's me!" I said proudly.

"The plants also can make having fun on the lake a lot harder and even cause problems with the dams", added Gary.

Hank was listening carefully. "This sounds like a big problem!" he said.

Gus sighed. "It is. The humans are working on the problem as best as they can. They are using special chemicals and special fish that like to eat it to fight the weeds."

"Oh! Hey there Chris! I was just talking about you!" Gary called out to a type of fish known as a carp. Chris was well hidden in the weedy invaders.

Gary said that he could talk about many more things, but we had to make it to the dam. He said we were getting close. Gary led the way and we fell in line behind him.

Then there it was. It was one of the largest man-made structures I had ever seen.

"Here we are! Welcome to the Dreher Shoals Dam!" Gary told us it was a little over 200 feet tall and about 1 ½ miles long.

"This is great. But I don't get it", asked Sammy. "What's the point?"

"I am glad you asked", Gary replied. Gary turned towards Hannah, Hank and I. He winked. "You three must have some sort of idea. Water has been around on Earth for a very long time. I will give you a hint: man uses water to do work."

My mind was churning with thoughts. Ah ha! I thought. "ME! ME! I have got it," I cried waving my hand in the air. "One side of the dam is higher than the other! Gravity pulls the water down from the high side to the lower side. The force of the water rushing down is used to make electricity! Literally the water is doing work!"

Hannah, Hank, Sammy and Gus stared at me wide-eyed. "I know what you are thinking," I said. "I lived inside of a physics teacher once though so this subject comes naturally to me," I said with a smile.

"So to get to the other side of the dam, I am guessing we have to go through this?" asked Hannah.

"Yes," said Gary. "But folks like you four do it all of the time. You will be fine! After this dam you will go through two more lakes and one more dam. Then you will be on the final leg of your journey. Be safe and it was nice meeting you!" Gary sent us on our way with these final words.

We were gathered around the entrance to the dam. We admitted we were nervous. The entrance (also called an **intake**) opened. We rushed in and DOWN. Smack! Smack! Oh no, I thought. Not this again. We were in the very front when the lake water was released so we were the first to slam into a large blade. It looked like the blade on a boat motor. The big blade pushed back. Slowly the blade began to move and pick up more speed. The force of the water was turning it. Just like a revolving door we were pushed through and past the blades and out of the dam.

Once outside we checked ourselves to make sure we were alright.

"Hey, that was better than any ride I have been on," summed up Hank.

"Well at least you weren't the one slamming your face into a giant metal blade," Hannah shot back.

I did my best to get in the middle of those two. They were always fighting! Right at that moment I noticed Sammy talking to someone. "Look, I wonder who that could be. She looks familiar."

She was much smaller than Sammy. She looked nice. She was also a bright, burnt orange color.

"Hey y'all, my name is Cassie. I am clay. You might have noticed my family and friends mixing with the rivers as you traveled downstream here in the Piedmont. You knocked me loose on your way into the canal when you left the dam. That's ok though, I will just travel with you for a bit," she said in a cheery voice. She had a lovely southern accent. She talked to us about the Saluda River. Sammy and Cassie seemed to really get along. I guess that is what you get when you get sediment together.

After leaving the dam, the Saluda River was very pleasant. The riverbanks were wooded. Rocks jutted out here and there. Once in a while we went through small rapids. Several times we passed people in kayaks fishing and paddling. It was so nice that we were surprised to see a shiny slick across the water in our path. We recognized it as oil.

"What is oil doing here, Cassie?" Sammy asked.

Cassie answered. "We are not too far from a major highway. When it rains, oil and other **pollution** on the road are washed into the river. It enters the river through storm drains. We call it **stormwater run-off**."

"That is just too bad", I said. I noticed a helpless fly caught in the oily mess.

Cassie told us more. "It doesn't just affect small animals like insects. It affects everybody. Animals of all sizes can eat it and get sick. It makes the water quality bad and unhealthy for plants, animals and humans. It can also get into the surrounding sediment. Nobody wins."

The scenery had now become more city-like. There were buildings and bridges and cars. We passed through the capitol of South Carolina, Columbia. We continued past the **fall line** as the Saluda River joined the Broad River and formed the Congaree River.

Part of the Congaree River is in the **sandhill region**. The sandhill region

has sandy soil where the ocean had at one time covered this part of the state. As the Congaree snaked through the sandhills and into the **flood plain**, we noticed looming canopies of cypress trees. We were on the edges of the swampland in Congaree National Park. The dark water was filled with life. We passed snakes, river otters and all sorts of birds.

We had now entered the **coastal plain**. The river slowed down a lot. In fact, it was getting wider. We were entering a very large swamp. Thanks to some helpful people we passed, we discovered we had entered the headwaters of Lake Marion.

From Lake Marion we would pass through a canal into Lake Moultrie. Then we would begin the final leg of our journey.

Vocabulary

- **abiotic** - something that is nonliving; an object that is not and was never living

- **biotic** - something that is living, or used to be alive

- **carnivore** –a consumer that eats only meat

- **coastal plain** – makes up 2/3 of South Carolina, flat land divided into the Inner and Outer Coastal Plain

- **ecosystem** - a given area that includes all the biotic and abiotic factors that interact with one another

- **fall line** – the boundary between the upstate and the lower part of the state, based on rocks and sediment types; at the fall line water moves from higher elevations to lower elevations sometime resulting in rapids

- **flood plain** – an area usually next to a river that can flood

- **fresh water** - water with a salinity of zero, meaning no salt

- **herbivore** - a consumer that eats only plants

- **hydroelectric dam** - a large structure that uses the potential energy of water   to produce electricity

- **intake** - controls the flow of water through the dam

- **native** – describes organisms that are part of an ecosystem through natural means (not introduced by humans)

- **pectoral fin** – fin (pair of fins) behind the fish's head, helps fish to swim

- **piedmont region** – a hilly region at the base of mountains

- **pollution** - any foreign substance that contaminates soil, air, or water; this   can occur by mixing or dissolving

- **producer** - an organism that can produce, or make, its own food

- **reservoir** - a man-made lake used to store water for a dam

- **sandhill region**– separates the piedmont from the coastal plain; formerly a coastline when the sea level was higher

- **saltwater** – found in the world's oceans, water that contains various types of salts

- **stormwater run-off** - created by rain falling on surfaces that prevent it from being absorbed into the ground (like roads and sidewalks); it can carry harmful pollutants

Did you know?

- The weedy plant that Gary the Garfish points out to everyone in the beginning of the chapter is an example of an invasive species. Invasive species are organisms that enter an area they are not native to. Because they are often able to successfully reproduce in large numbers, they begin to out-compete plants or animals that already live in the area. They can use up vital resources such as food, space, and in this case, even dissolved oxygen.

- Stormwater runoff can carry with it all sorts of pollutants, both natural and man- made. We call these pollutants non-point source pollutants, because they do not come from one particular source but many. Paved roads, driveways, parking lots, and sidewalks can increase non-point source pollution in bodies of water by not allowing stormwater to be absorbed by soil, but instead to make it to a river, lake, or stream.

- As the Congaree River snakes its way past cypress trees and around swamps, the water is described as dark. This is because of chemicals called tannins that are leached into the water by the cypress trees, as well as decaying plant material.

Points to Ponder

1. Can you illustrate the food chain that is discussed by Gary the Garfish?

2. What is the most important force that a dam takes advantage of?

3. Can you think of any ways to reduce non-point source pollution in your neighborhood?

Where are Oscar & his friends now?

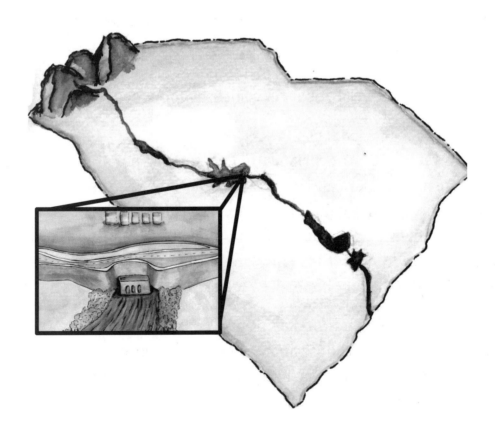

Making the Connection:

History, Science and South Carolina Go Hand in Hand

The Saluda River was dammed in 1930 to form a reservoir that would supply upstate South Carolina residents with electricity. By blocking the flow of a river, water piles up against the upstream side of the dam, while downstream of the dam water levels are drastically reduced. The water in the lake is being held back by the dam, and should the dam break, water would rush down and out of the reservoir with the force of gravity.

People take advantage of the water's gravitational potential energy (the idea that the water is sitting on the top of a hill) by regulating the flow of that water through an intake (entrance water can flow through) and directing it to a turbine. The moment water is released through the intake and into the penstock (the canal that leads to the turbine), its potential energy has been converted to kinetic energy (the energy of motion) by the force of gravity. As the water rushes into the turbine blades, the unbalanced force of the water on those blades causes them to spin forward. This, in turn, rotates a shaft that is in a generator. A generator is a type of motor or engine. The generator creates electricity using magnetic forces. That electricity is used to light up thousands of homes.

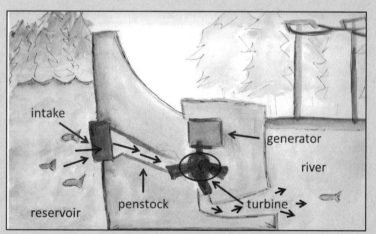

However, Lake Murray has been used for more than generating electricity. After Japan attacked Pearl Harbor during World War II (1941), the United States needed a serious confidence boost. The Doolittle Raid of 1942 was the answer. It was the first air raid on Japan during the war. While it did not dramatically damage Japan, it served its purpose by bolstering American morale.

The 17th Bomb Group was selected to carry out the mission, and part of their training took place in South Carolina over Lake Murray. They practiced very short take-offs like those from an aircraft carrier and aimed at practice targets in the lake. When they left for their secret mission over Japan, back-up flight crews continued to train over the lake. Unfortunately, five of the B-25 Bombers that were flown in these practices crashed and sank. Most were recovered.

B-25 Bombers used a radial combustion engine to turn their propellers, so the plane could take flight. Combustion engines are found in cars, motorcycles, trains and planes. If you rode in a car or bus, today, you used a machine that converts chemical energy into mechanical energy. And wouldn't you know it? Oxygen and water are involved yet again!

Combustion is a chemical reaction where oxygen gas reacts with a fuel to rapidly release heat while producing water and carbon dioxide. Another way to say this is that fuel and oxygen gas go through a chemical change. The heat that is produced causes gas to expand and apply a force that causes the engine to crank. Similar to the hydroelectric dam, force and motion are used to operate an engine. That engine turns the propeller blades on the airplane which will help it to fly.

Chapter 6

Carolina Coast,

"Here we are everyone! Lake Marion!" said an excited Cassie. "I have heard so much about it from my friends."

Sammy said he wished we had someone like Gary to show us around. "We might get lost without a guide."

I agreed. "This place is huge."

Cassie told us that Lake Marion is the largest lake in South Carolina. It is so large that some call it an inland sea. We all kept our eyes peeled for anybody that looked like they could help us with directions. We spotted a black and white striped fish proudly swimming in our direction. We flagged him down.

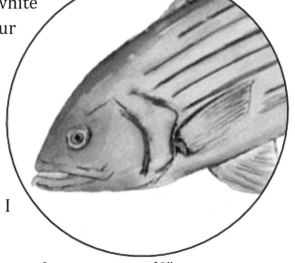

"Excuse us, sir. Can you spare a moment?" Cassie called out politely.

The fish was absorbed in his thoughts. He looked up and was startled to see us. "What was that? I didn't hear you."

I piped up. "We are new here. Can you show us around?"

"Well, I was on my way to an important ceremony, but it isn't for a few more hours. I guess I could spare some time," said the fish. He turned around and asked us to keep up with him.

Even though we had been through lakes and drifted down several rivers, this was the first time I started to take in the sights. I looked from side to side and beneath us. I noticed small plant-like organisms everywhere, but mostly at the surface. They were microscopic compared to the fish but many times larger than Hank, Hannah and I. I had seen these before in my travels all over the world, but did not know much about them. I could see they were carried by the current. Some were pointy. Some were round like a ball. Some even had what looked like tails whipping back and forth. I decided I would definitely ask our guide about these later.

I am sorry I didn't introduce myself earlier. My name is Bob," said our leader. I am a striped bass, but I am sure you have heard of me before."

"Actually, I haven't. Have you?" I asked my friends. Everyone shook their heads no, including Cassie and Sammy.

Bob looked a little shocked. He also looked disappointed. "I am truly surprised. The Santee River was dammed in 1941 to create Lake Marion and Lake Moultrie. When the river was dammed, a group of striped bass became trapped in the lakes. Usually part of the striped bass life cycle takes place in the ocean. My relatives survived to become the first striped bass that lived entirely in fresh water, inland! We are famous! We have a ceremony each year to recognize ourselves and this wonderful achievement. I am giving a speech today."

We all congratulated Bob. We were lucky to come across him. What an interesting story.

"Was the Santee River dammed for the same reason the Saluda River was dammed?" asked a curious Cassie.

"I hear it is a similar story," said Bob. During the 1930's there was a time called the Great Depression. During the Depression jobs were hard to find and living from day to day was hard. There also was no electricity in the area. So the lives of people in the Santee River Basin would be better, the river was dammed so that people could have jobs and electricity. Lake Marion and Lake Moultrie were created as **reservoirs** to supply dams with water to make electricity. To flood the basin the area was evacuated. Communities were moved and buildings were knocked down or flooded. Today people visit the lakes to enjoy being outside."

Hannah pointed out that people were everywhere.

"You are right. There are people fishing, water skiing and camping! Look, there are a bunch of kids on the lake shore over there," I said.

"Those are summer campers learning about our ecosystem. They come every year," explained Bob.

"Do you mind if we swim over and listen to what they are learning?" I asked. Bob said he thought we had enough time.

"Listen up class," the teacher was saying. "Today we are going to discuss the connection between sunlight, oxygen and the **producers** in Lake Marion."

Between snippets of their conversation I learned that the many small plant-like organisms I saw were **phytoplankton**. Like the blueberry bush Sammy and his family had clung to, phytoplankton use energy from the sun to produce their own food. Living things that make their own food are called producers. If a living thing cannot make its own food it has to eat it and is called a **consumer**. The deer that ate the bush and the trout that ate the nymph were both consumers. All of the energy in the lake ecosystem comes from the sun and the producers that can transform sunlight to useful energy for themselves and others.

A little boy in the group on the shore raised his hand. He was very excited. "That means phytoplankton are really important! All of the plants here are important!"

"This is correct," said the teacher.

Their lesson got even more interesting. They talked about oxygen! Of course that made me happy. I learned that when plants make food from sunlight they give off oxygen gas!

The teacher kept talking. "Some of that gas stays in the water. It is **dissolved**. Some of that gas goes into the air. When it is in the air animals with lungs and humans breathe it." I was really enjoying learning all of this.

Bob snapped me back into reality. He said it was time to go. We waved good-bye to Bob at the entrance to the canal. This canal would take us from Lake Marion to Lake Moultrie.

Suddenly, a boat roared past us! We all flew into the air! While flipping above the lake I noticed the blurry faces of frightened oxygen molecules mixed in with us. We all splashed back into the lake below.

"Wow! Are you OK?" I asked a pair of oxygens next to me.

We are fine, just a bit of a rough landing. Looks like we will be hanging out in the lake water for a while," they answered.

"You can do that?" asked Hannah.

"Yes we can. Some of the oxygen gas dissolved in the lake comes from producers. Some comes from the air," said the oxygens.

I had just learned this. I felt like I was starting to put two and two together. Everything really is connected! The water and the air above the lake are connected too!

At that time, a very large building on the water came into view. "Uh-oh, here we go again," said Hank.

"Yes, I would be very happy if we weren't right in the front this time," added Hannah. "I don't feel like crashing into those blades again."

So we waited outside, ready to enter the Pinopolis Dam. This time the ride was much smoother.

Vocabulary
- **consumer** – organisms that must eat food to have energy to live and grow

- **phytoplankton** - plant-like plankton can be single or multi-celled and use photosynthesis to produce their own food

- **plankton** - organisms that drift; organisms that cannot actively swim and are pushed by currents and waves

- **producers** – produce their own food to be used for energy to live and grow, they form the bottom of the food chain

- **reservoir** – a body of water used for a water supply

Did you know?

- Striped bass are anadromous fish, meaning they are born in freshwater, spend their lives in salt water, and return to freshwater to reproduce. Other anadromous fish include herring, sturgeon, and salmon. While we do not have salmon in South Carolina, we do have herring and sturgeon. Because the dam blocked the river, a fish lift has been built at Lake Moultrie. St. Stephen's fish lift is much like an elevator, allowing the fish to pass through the dam!

Points to Ponder

1. Phytoplankton play important roles, not only in the immediate ecosystems they are a part of, but on a global scale as well! They are responsible for over 70% of the oxygen on Earth!

2. In what ways would the removal of phytoplankton affect a food chain and an ecosystem?

Where are Oscar & his friends now?

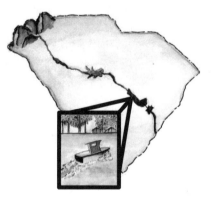

Chapter 7

Into the Estuary!

Arrival in Charleston Harbor

We were exhausted. It had been a long journey. The last trip through the dam had worn us all out. The sun was setting. The movement of the river was rocking us to sleep.

We woke up the next morning to the sound of birds. They were squawking as they flew overhead. We rubbed our eyes and opened them to a new day. There was so much to see. We saw factories. Their smoke stacks were puffing out clouds of smoke and steam. There were a lot of buildings, parking lots and pavement dotted here and there with pine trees and shrubs. I shouted up to what looked like a vulture. It was circling over the riverbank. "Where are we?"

"Y'all are in the Cooper River. You aren't too far from Charleston Harbor," the vulture shouted back.

"This is so cool! We are almost to the coast!" said Hank and Hannah.

"I think you two are right," said Cassie. "We are flowing through a region called the **coastal zone**. Soon there should be clues to tell us just how close we are to the ocean."

"I think we should relax. I would like to sit back and take in the sights. We have traveled so far," I said.

Sammy agreed. So the five of us floated downstream and enjoyed our surroundings.

The first thing I noticed were the oxygen gas molecules in the water. Just like I learned in Lake Marion, I watched oxygen gas entering the air from the water. I also saw it mix in with the water from the air.

The second thing I noticed was the heat. It was very hot outside. A fish swimming below yelled up to us that the water was cooler where he was. "Don't forget to wear sunscreen!" he reminded us.

The top layer of water was so warm that I saw water molecules **evaporating**. I had evaporated with Hank and Hannah many times before, but had not noticed it until now on our trip.

There was so much going on! The water was also very murky. It had a lot of dirt in it. I saw the silt and sediment traveling near us say hi to Sammy and Cassie. Phytoplankton surrounded us, hanging out near the surface. Microscopic animals floating in the water fed on each other and on the phytoplankton. I saw atoms mixed in with the water. Sometimes they were alone. Sometimes they were joined with others forming molecules.

Once again, we talked about how nice one last guide would be. We did not have to wait long. The best part was, this time they were almost my size! I heard them joking before I saw them.

"Knock, knock," said one.

"Who's there?" said the other.

"Tide."

"Tide who?"

"Tide rather be downstream!" They burst into fits of loud laughter. They were laughing so hard they almost slammed right into us.

"Oh dear, I am so sorry." He was speaking through tears and gasps of breath. "I am Nick, a **sodium ion**. This is Clarence, he is a **chloride ion**."

"I'm Oscar. I am oxygen. My friends Hank and Hannah are hydrogen. Joined together we are water."

"We are dissolved in water, but together we are salt," said Nick.

I have seen atoms like you two in the ocean before. What are you doing in the river?" asked Hank.

"That is a great question! If you hang on for a bit we will show you," replied the two friends.

We traveled a little farther. We noticed large ships. Some carried big containers filled with all kinds of stuff. Other ships were under tall cranes. The cranes were moving the containers off and on. I wondered what was happening. Nick said that  water is used for many things. It is used to make electricity like we saw at the dams. It is also used for moving goods all over the world. These things will be unloaded, bought and sold. Some of these huge ships traveled thousands of miles to make their deliveries.

We traveled under bridges and closer to the shore. We discovered differences from earlier. First, we weren't flowing quickly at all. In fact, I had to try hard to swim forward. If I didn't swim forward I was pushed backwards. Second, Nick and Clarence had friends everywhere. We met more sodiums and chlorides the more we swam.

Nick said I was a good observation maker. He also said that the reason we were swimming forward and seeing more salt was because of the **tides**. Tides are caused by gravity. Gravity from the moon and the sun pull on the water that is on Earth. We experience tides on Earth as a rise and fall of water. During high tide, water from the ocean creeps inland.

"So that explains it!" I cried. "We are being pushed backwards because it is becoming high tide! Ocean water is moving into the river. That is also why we are seeing more salt!"

"That's right," said Nick and Clarence. "The closer we get to the ocean, the more of us you will see."

We passed slowly under the Cooper River Bridge. It is also known as the Arthur Ravenel Jr. Bridge. We decided to stop swimming against the tide and rest. We ducked behind a buoy. The water rushed past on either side.

Now that we weren't moving I looked around some more. There was a lot going on in and out of the water. Fish and dolphins were swimming all around us. Pelicans hovered above. They looked into the water below for their next meal. It was at this moment I observed something really neat. Animals and plants were giving off and using molecules, like oxygen gas and **carbon dioxide**. I had seen this before but I had never been a part of it. Maybe I would get a chance later.

Nick and Clarence told us where we were. We had made it to Charleston Harbor. Three rivers, the Ashley, Cooper and Wando, meet the Atlantic Ocean here. This type of ecosystem is called an **estuary**. An estuary is where fresh water from land mixes with salty water from the ocean. Water in an estuary is called **brackish**. Brackish water is saltier than freshwater but not as salty as ocean water.

Just like the streams, rivers and lakes we had been to, all of the biotic and abiotic factors in this area are connected. Clarence said he had a great example of this around an **aircraft carrier**.

As soon as the tide started to go out we rode with it to the ship. There she stood. She was steely gray. She towered over us and was nearly 900 feet long.

"Here we are! This is the USS Yorktown! This aircraft carrier was built in the 1940s and used during WWII and Vietnam. Tourists come from all over to see where sailors made the ultimate sacrifice," our new friends told us.

"So it is like a floating museum," said Sammy.

"Not quite," said Nick. "It is actually stuck in the mud almost 30 feet deep! The humans put it in the mud on purpose, so that it wouldn't move. But there is more to that story. Sammy and Cassie, you both were eroded upstream, right? Then you were taken by water downstream."

Sammy and Cassie nodded.

"You two are not alone," continued Nick. "These rivers bring tons of sand, **silt** and clay to the harbor. Then all of that sediment is **deposited**. Sometimes it forms sand bars. Sometimes it rests next to the Yorktown, or in a marsh or even **barrier islands** and beaches."

The light came on in Sammy's eyes. "That is what happened to Gus! He was deposited in a river!"

"When will we be deposited?" asked Sammy.

Clarence shrugged. He said he was not sure. It depended on the movement of the water. If it slowed down enough Sammy and Cassie would settle somewhere.

I turned my attention on the USS Yorktown. Looking at the side of the ship gave us a lot of information. Oysters, algae and barnacles made up the **community** on the **hull**. These neat animals and plants were attached to the side. Nick explained that because they don't move they are called **sessile**. They only lived part way up the hull. Where they stopped living marked where the water rose to on a high tide. I could also see a high tide line on the pilings near the docks and on the salt marsh grass.

Nick also thought seeing the oysters on the ship was interesting. He said it reminded him of how humans and the other animals, and even plants, are connected.

We swam over to the Yorktown to take a closer look. On our way, we passed a diamondback terrapin swimming to the marsh grass. Nick called out and waved, "Hi Tiny!"

Seagulls flew over a pier with clams in their beaks. They dropped them onto the pavement below. They smashed open and the gulls picked out the sweet meat.

Underneath the pier Clarence pointed out a **sheepshead** and a stone crab hanging out in an old milk crate. We saw a large snail that Nick called a **whelk**. Nick said that whelks and stone crabs were predators that liked to eat animals like oysters and clams.

Out of nowhere Hannah screamed!

A shadowy figure was way to close. A large claw rocked closer. "Boo!" shouted Nick. "I got you guys!"

Nick and Clarence were behind the crab claw laughing. "No worries! It is just an **exoskeleton**! Animals like crabs and shrimp have them. They shed them when they grow. And look! There are bacteria all over this claw. They are breaking it down! **Decomposers** like bacteria are my favorite part of the food chain," said Nick with a wink.

We were finally right up next to the edge of the Yorktown. The ship was sharp and jagged with oysters and barnacles. They were everywhere. Clarence said they were very different animals but both begin their life as

zooplankton. As they get older they land on a hard surface and stay for the rest of their lives.

I was listening to Clarence. I was also paying attention to the oysters. We were getting too close to the action. The oysters and barnacles were feeding. Their mouth parts and legs and all sorts of things were sucking and whirring. It was stirring the water with us in it all up. We didn't realize until it was too late that Hank, Hannah and I were on a path to collide with a large, green **diatom**.

Vocabulary

- **aircraft carrier** – a ship designed to launch and land aircraft like planes

- **barrier island** - a coastal island separated from the mainland by water and salt marsh; it serves as a barrier (protection) for the land from storms and flooding

- **brackish water** - water that is a mixture of fresh and salt water resulting in salinity higher than freshwater but lower than the average salinity of the ocean

- **carbon dioxide** – a gas made of carbon and oxygen that is given off during biological reactions

- **community** – different kinds of organisms that live in the same area together form a community

- **decomposer** - an organism (bacteria, mushrooms, earthworms) that recycles dead and decaying matter back into its elemental building blocks

- **deposited** – when sediment that has been eroded settles; deposition (the process of depositing) builds landforms

- **diatom** - plant-like plankton (phytoplankton) with a hard, glass-like outer layer; can be single-celled or multi-celled and come in a variety of shapes and sizes

- **estuary** - an ecosystem where freshwater rivers meet the ocean; characterized by brackish water

- **exoskeleton** - a tough outer skeleton that is regularly molted (shed) as the animal grows; characteristic of organisms such as shrimp, crabs and barnacles

- **hull** – the body of a boat or ship excluding the deck or structures on the deck

- **ion** - an atom with an electrical charge

- **sessile** – not moving; in this case organisms that are attached to a surface and do not move

- **sheepshead** – type of fish found in brackish or salt water with bold black and white vertical stripes

- **silt** - soil particles that are smaller than sand but larger than clay; has a fine, smooth texture

- **tide** - the gravitational pull of the moon and the sun on the Earth's hydrosphere (the band of water on Earth)

- **whelk** – a snail that is found in brackish and salt water

- **zooplankton** - animal plankton; they are consumers and can be carnivores, herbivores, or omnivores; some are the juvenile stages of marine organisms

Did you know?

- Phytoplankton are restricted to the photic zone in the water. The photic zone is the top portion of the water that receives enough light for a plant to photosynthesize. In other words, photosynthesizers cannot survive in deeper, darker water.

- Solutions are most often solids dissolved in liquids, gases dissolved in liquids, and liquids mixed with other liquids. In the case of salt water, solid salt is dissolved in the liquid phase of water. The substance dissolving in the liquid is the solute. The liquid that dissolves the solute is called the solvent. The defining characteristic of a solution is that the solute is distributed evenly throughout the solvent.

- The concentration of a solution is how much solute is dissolved in your solvent. The more salt dissolved in water, the higher the concentration. Ocean water has a higher concentration of salt than brackish water. Brackish water has a higher concentration of salt than freshwater.

Points to Ponder

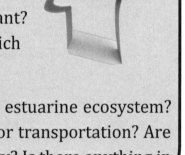

1. Can you list all of the biotic and abiotic factors found in this chapter?

2. Based on what you have read so far, what are the ways in which too much sediment could impact an ecosystem negatively and be considered a pollutant? (hint: sediment affects the turbidity of water, which means that it makes the water murky)

3. What are the ways that humans interact with this estuarine ecosystem? Do they just use it for recreation? Do they use it for transportation? Are humans a part of the food chain found in an estuary? Is there anything in this estuary that humans depend on?

Where are Oscar & his friends now?

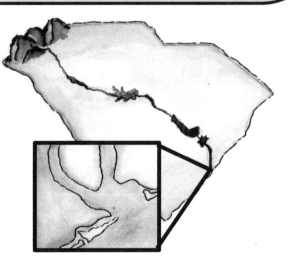

Chapter 8

One Final Detour

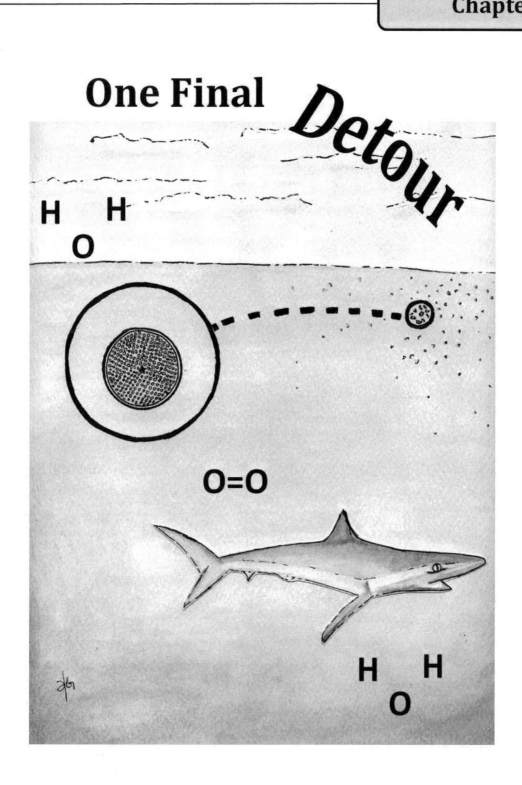

Here is what happened next. Hank, Hannah and I made it INSIDE of **single-celled phytoplankton**! We had no idea what was going on. Hannah was screaming. Hank was screaming. I had my eyes shut. Are you kidding me? We traveled all of this way to end up in what looked like a big green circle?

This was not cool. But it turned out a lot was going on in this green diatom. After all, a cell is the smallest unit of life. Inside of a cell there are actually many different jobs to be done. These jobs are in different places inside the cell. Wouldn't you know it? We were where a lot of photosynthesis happened.

Things were a blur. I was separated from Hank and Hannah. I called out to them. There was no response. The next thing I knew I was paired up with an oxygen atom. We were released from the cell into the water as oxygen gas!

"Whoah! That was crazy!" I shouted.

"Hi, I am Ozzy," said the oxygen atom. "You haven't done that before? I have done it hundreds of times. Now other organisms can use us in a different way. You see, we were just used in photosynthesis. Photosynthesis builds molecules to be used as energy. Now we can be used in the opposite process. We can be a part of breaking down molecules to release that energy." Like everyone else I had met, Ozzy really knew what he was talking about.

"That is all fine and dandy, but I lost my friends Hank and Hannah!" I said.

"Don't worry. They could have been used for a variety of things. If you're lucky, you might see them again!"

That would be wonderful. I imagined us all together again. I was busy imagining us floating on a gentle ocean breeze, like before the storm, when Ozzy and I entered the GILLS OF A SHARK!

The gills of a shark! Why did these things keep happening to me? From the gills we entered the bloodstream and met blood cells. The blood cells took us to a cell that needed oxygen to help break down other molecules.

After that, Ozzy was replaced with two hydrogen atoms (can I not keep a friend around here?!). I returned with them to the surrounding water as a, well, a water molecule. Whew! I was tired!

But that is when the light bulb went off over my head (ding!). Matter is recycled! Everything in this ecosystem is much more connected than I ever imagined! You see, we traveled across an entire ocean. We then rained down onto the mountain region of South Carolina. We entered rivers, lakes and an estuary. Everywhere we traveled was connected by us- by WATER!

All of our friends in the Blue Ridge region are connected to our buddies in the piedmont, sandhills, coastal plain and coastal zone. Everyone is part of one large **watershed** extending from the mountains to the ocean! Not only is everyone and everything joined by our watery geography, but by biology too.

Hannah, Hank and I linked the vast ocean to majestic mountains to individual cells! If that isn't amazing, I don't know what is. And with that I was ready to head back to the Atlantic.

Vocabulary

- **single-celled plankton** – plankton made up of only one cell

- **watershed** - an area where all water drains to a common source

Did you know?

- The ingredients for photosynthesis are water (H_2O), carbon dioxide (CO_2), and light. In the end, the plant makes sugars. As a byproduct, it releases oxygen gas (O_2).

- All cells in all living things need energy. One way to get that energy is a process called cellular respiration. In many organisms, cellular respiration requires oxygen to help break down molecules for energy. a byproduct of cellular respiration is water.

- There are many ways to divide South Carolina into watersheds. You could say that all of South Carolina is one large watershed where water flows from the mountains to the ocean. Some people prefer to divide South Carolina into smaller watersheds. According to the South Carolina Department of Natural Resources, we can divide the state into 4 major watersheds: Savannah, ACE, Santee, and Pee Dee.

Points to Ponder

Do you know what watershed you live in? In what watersheds did Oscar's journey take place? One good link for exploring South Carolina's watersheds is:

http://www.dnr.sc.gov/water/envaff/river/map.html.

So This is How it Ends

I was drifting with the tide. It was pulling me towards the ocean with my new friends Harry and Heather. We passed Fort Sumter on our right. Sullivan's Island was to our left. Waves crashed like music on the beaches and palm trees bent in the wind.

"Did you hear that?" I asked the two hydrogens.

"No, what was it?"

"I am sure I heard my name. That is so strange!" I said.

I heard it again. Then I spotted them! Cassie and Sammy were on the beach! They had finally been deposited! They looked happy. They waved to us as the swift current moved us out of the channel.

Wait. Did I hear my name again?

I turned and saw Hank and Hannah! They had made it out of the diatom! They were swept toward us. I could see they had a new oxygen friend with them.

"This is Oliver!" they told me excitedly.

We chatted and chatted. We were overjoyed to reunite. We discussed all of the things we saw on our adventure. We also talked about our new understanding of the world and the way it worked. We promised to stay in touch as we drifted out into the Atlantic.

Who knew where we would end up? Maybe in the Gulf Stream? Maybe we would make it to Africa again. But I will tell you this: we are all still here on Earth, getting recycled over and over. And maybe, just maybe, I am sitting writing this story from somewhere inside of YOU.

Did you know?

Because of our Earth's rotation, any object moving over the Earth's surface (like water) appears to be deflected to the right in the Northern Hemisphere and to the left in the Southern Hemisphere. This effect is in part responsible for the Gulf Stream moving north along the East Coast of the United States, then turning and crossing the Atlantic and traveling back south along the coast of Africa towards the equator.

Points to Ponder

Take the Oscar Challenge

Take a look around you. It can be hard to imagine all the ways in which biotic and abiotic factors are connected. There are so many! Choose an ecosystem like your schoolyard, your neighborhood, the beach, or even your backyard. Can you list all of the biotic and abiotic factors? Oscar challenges you to describe or illustrate in a chart all of the ways in which everything is connected based on all of your newfound knowledge.

CHAPTERS ONE & TWO

Extensions

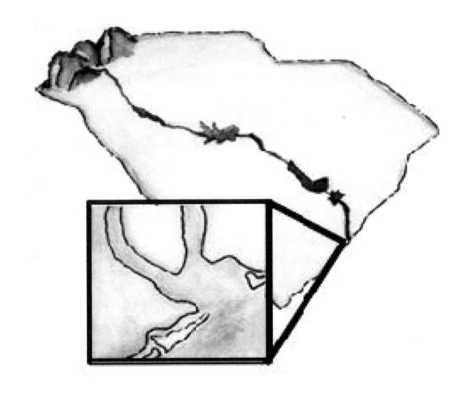

Matter Matters!

Fill in the blank with either: **solid**, **liquid** *or* **gas**

1) Oscar, Hank and Hannah as water vapor are_____.

2) Clouds are made up of tiny_____droplets.

3) Rain drops are_____.

4) A feather is a_____.

5) Oscar, Hank and Hannah as a cloud in a hurricane are_____drops.

Do you know as much as Oscar about matter? Match the state of matter on the left with its definition in the middle and its picture on the right!

Solid

a) This state of matter has a definite shape and volume.

Liquid

b) This state of matter will fill an entire container! It has NO definite shape or volume.

Gas

c) This state of matter has a definite volume but no definite shape – it will take the shape of its container.

Making the Connection

Wind and Weather *Matter*!

Oscar and his friends experienced several natural events in Chapter 2. They changed from a gaseous state of matter to a liquid state while blowing around in our atmosphere and as part of a thunderstorm that was destined to become a hurricane.

It can be hard to imagine all of the matter around us, especially when it comes to the gases that make up our atmosphere. Gentle breezes and gusts of wind are reminders that there is more around us than meets the eye.

Where does wind come from?

Our Sun heats Earth unevenly. Some places are heated more than others. When gases in our atmosphere are heated, they rise. As warm air rises, cooler air travels to take its place. This movement can be felt as wind. Warm air that has moved upward becomes cool. Cooler air sinks. Because of the warm air rising, the cooler air must travel away to move downward. We also feel that as wind. This cycle happens on small scales and big scales. It happens on the beach as a "sea breeze" and on a global scale, too.

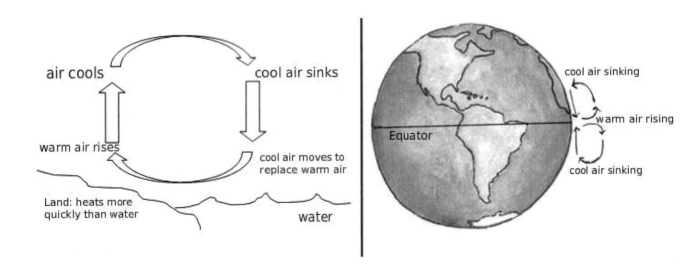

Gases and Temperature

All of the above sounds great, but why does warm air rise and cool air sink? When a gas is heated, the molecules spread out as the temperature increases. When a gas is cooled, the molecules stay closer together, causing the gas to sink.

Wind in Motion: How do we describe wind?

Two ways we can describe wind and its motion are speed and direction. Wind speed is the time it takes for wind to travel a specific distance. There are tools available to measure speed. Wind speed is important to us because high wind speeds can damage homes and other buildings and even put our lives in danger during extreme weather events.

Wind direction describes where wind is coming from. A "North wind" describes wind coming from the north and blowing south. Sailors, pilots and kite flyers are just some of the many people interested in wind direction. We can determine wind direction from high tech equipment but also objects as simple as wind socks, wind vanes and flags. At the end of this section are directions on how to build and use your own wind vane.

What did the weatherman say?

Often on the news, we hear the weather anchor (the person who delivers the weather on television) talk about areas of high and low pressure. Areas where cool air is sinking are described as high pressure areas. Places experiencing high pressure have fair, sunny and dry weather. Areas where warm area is rising, like near the equator, are considered areas of low pressure. Rainy, cloudy weather is associated with low pressure. Hurricanes, like the one Oscar, Hank and Hannah become a part of, form in low pressure areas where warm moist air is rising and creating thunderstorms.

Activity 1: Make your own wind vane:

Materials:

Paper plate

Pipe
cleaner

Straw

Yarn/string (approx. 5
inches) Scissors

Marker

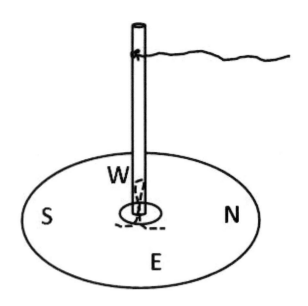

Directions:

1. Cut a slit in the center of paper plate.

2. Fold pipe cleaner in half and insert ends through slit approximately 1/3 of the pipe cleaner's length with the plate "upside down" (the "eating side" is facing down).

3. Separate the ends to anchor the pipe cleaner to the plate.

4. Slide the straw over the protruding pipe cleaner on the top side of the plate.

5. Label the four cardinal points (N, E, S, W) at 90° angles to one another.

6. Tie yarn tightly to top of straw.

How it works:

As mentioned above, wind is described in terms of the direction it comes from. Take your wind vane outside and position it so the N is pointed north. (It is easiest to observe wind direction on a hard, flat surface you can hold your plate still on.) **Your "tell-tale" or piece of yarn will blow in the direction that is opposite from where the wind is blowing from.** Your tell-tale can also give you an idea of relative wind strength; if the yarn is blowing straight back, the wind is blowing harder than if the yarn is blowing back at an angle.

Activity 2: Wind vane Warm-Up:

Let's practice with the <u>wind vane </u>pictured on the previous page and the <u>illustration </u>shown below:

1) According to the wind vane pictured above, what direction is the wind coming from?

2) According to the picture below, which direction is the helicopter traveling? Is it headed N, S, E or W? What direction is the sailboat traveling?

3) Is the sailboat heading into the wind, or away from it?

4) What about the helicopter? Is it heading away from or into the wind?

5) Do you think the force of the wind on the helicopter is going to speed it up or slow it down? Why or why not? What about the sailboat? Is the wind pushing with it or against it? Will this speed up the sailboat or slow it down? If you have discussed force and motion with your class, use what you know about unbalanced forces and apply it to the illustration.

Activity 3: Use Your Wind vane

With an adult take your wind vane outside. Watch how it moves and answer the questions below.

What direction is the wind coming from?

Is it blowing hard or gently?

What other observations can you make?

Activity 4: Hurricane Tracking

Begin tracking Oscar's Hurricane using the latitude and longitude below. You can print a hurricane tracking chart from:

http://www.nhc.noaa.gov/pdf/tracking_chart_atlantic.pdf

Day	Latitude	Longitude
1	13°N	23°W
2	12°N	28°W
3	12°N	34°W
4	13°N	44°W

CHAPTER THREE

Extensions

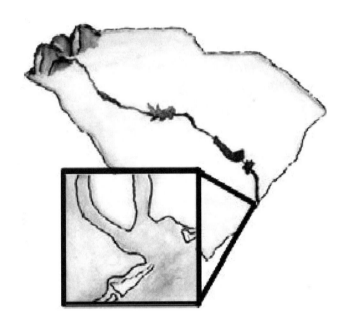

Making the Connection

Bracing for Impact

Constructive and destructive processes occur all over our planet Earth, building landforms, breaking them down, and building them again. Sometimes these events are natural and sometimes they are influenced by humans.

Hurricanes are powerful natural events that can bring with them damaging heavy rain and strong winds. In Chapter 3, Oscar, Hank and Hannah make landfall as a hurricane and rain down on the Mountain Region of South Carolina. As they crash down onto Table Rock they break off a tiny piece of the rock face; this is an example of erosion. Erosion can happen during hurricanes due to wind, rain, flooding and storm surge.

Damage due to hurricanes is usually the worst on the coast. Beaches and barrier islands take the full force of the storm before it begins to weaken as it moves inland. Hurricanes and even smaller storms can dramatically change coastal scenery very quickly. Sand from beaches is sometimes washed out to sea or even washed inland into buffering maritime forest and marshes. What used to be a gently sloping beach face can become a narrow, steep beach face broken up by ledges and drop-offs.

Wind and rain can be destructive, but the most damage is typically due to storm surge. On the East Coast of the United States, hurricane winds push water inland from the Atlantic Ocean. Storm surge can flood homes and streets from a few inches to many feet.

Today, with more people moving to coastal areas than ever before, it is important to understand hurricanes. This knowledge provides us with information on how to stay safe, evacuate and protect our belongings.

Activity 1: Beach Profiles: A Closer Look at Beach Face Shape

It is important to monitor and record beach shape and the way beaches change over time. This can help us predict beach shape in the future and after storm events.

Check out the following beach profile. It is sort of like looking at a slice of the beach from the side.

Stop and think. What is a profile? Everyone has one... even the beach!

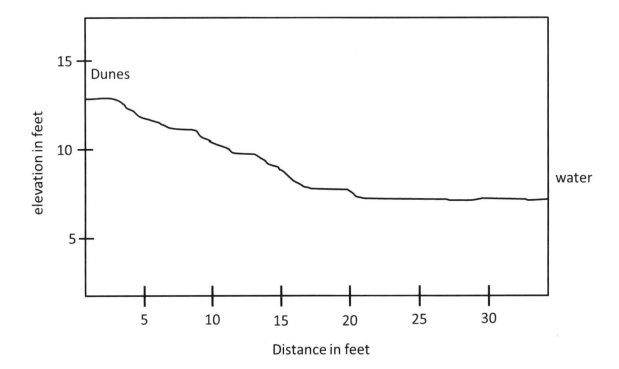

The previous page is an example of a beach profile. Now it is your turn! Graph the ordered pairs below onto the blank profile graph and connect the points with a line.

(0, 12)

(5, 10)

(10, 6)

(15, 5)

(20, 3)

(25, 3)

(30, 3)

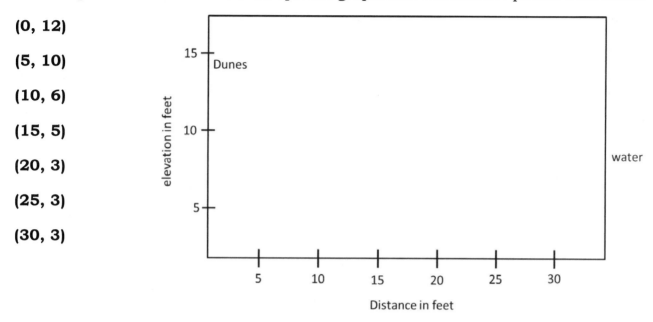

Idea: You can trace the large beach profile graph with tracing paper and use it as a template for your beach profile. When you are complete you can lay your graph over the original profile to compare!

What profile might show the beach after a storm? Why?

Activity 2: Finish Tracking Oscar's Storm!

Day	Latitude	Longitude
5	15°N	53°W
6	18°N	60°W
7	22°N	67°W
8	25°N	73°W
9	30°N	77°W
10	32°N	80°W

Where do Oscar, Hank and Hannah end up?

CHAPTER FOUR

Extensions

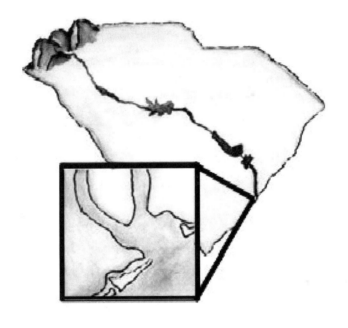

Making the Connection

Trout, Timber and Turbidity!

Oscar, Hank and Hannah have made many friends so far along their journey! Can you recall how many new characters have been introduced so far?

At the beginning of the chapter the tiny group is floating downstream and has a close encounter with a toothy, scaled predator about to make a meal out of an insect. Fortunately the group drifted past the hungry **brook trout** just in time.

Brook trout are a type of fish known as char. They are found in clear cold streams - exactly the kind of streams found in the Blue Ridge region of South Carolina. Brook trout are special as they are the only trout* native to South Carolina. However, while their story is now hopeful, it hasn't always been.

South Carolina has a variety of natural resources (a resource that exists in nature and can be useful and valuable to humans). One of these resources is timber. Timber is wood that will be used for things like building or carpentry. Beginning in the 1800s loggers cut down many of the forests in the Blue Ridge region. This was bad news for trout for many reasons.

Stop and think.
Brainstorm by yourself or with a group about why this was bad news for the brook trout.

Forests provide shade for streams. With no shade the water was warmed by the sun to temperatures that the trout could not survive in.

Now recall what you learned in Chapter 3 and your Chapter 3 extensions. What job do trees, shrubs and other plants do to protect land and landforms from destructive processes like erosion? Their roots hold dirt in place! With no more trees is a forest rain easily washes away dirt into nearby streams making them cloudy and murky.

Remember that trouts like cold *clear* streams. The heavy *sedimentation* of mountain streams pushed out the trout. In this case the sediment acts as pollution.

To make matters worse, to re-supply the streams with trout, humans introduced rainbow trout and brown trout. These two types of trout were able to out-compete the native brook trout.

Can you explain how the idea of limiting factors might relate to this **situation?**

Why do you think it important to protect the factors that make up an ecosystem, like the brook trout?

Today, with raised awareness and education the brook trout is doing better. Companies that log are using more environmentally-friendly practices and kids like you are learning about protecting the trout in classrooms! There are even programs that raise brook trout and release them into just the right kind of mountin streams.

These are just a few examples of how humans affect and impact our planet in both negative and positive ways.

Activity 1: Check Your Comprehension!

Using the table below, list the human activities mentioned in the readings above as either positive or negative for the brook trout. Add rows if you need to!

Human Activity	Positive or Negative?	Describe

Activity 2: Murky Measurements

Make Your Own Secchi Disk

When scientists talk about how clear a body or sample of water is, the use the word turbidity. Turbidity is a measure of how much "stuff", like dirt, is in the water based on how murky (a good word to use here is opaque, an antonym of the word clear) the water is. As you learned already, certain animals like trout can not live in turbid water. When land is deforested, then eroded and that sediment becomes suspended or deposited in a small stream it is no longer suitable for a brook trout to live in.

How do scientists measure turbidity? One of the simple ways is to use a secchi disk. Secchi disks are a circular disk painted in an alternating black and white pattern with a rope that is marked off in units of the users choice. The disk is lowered into the water, and once it can no longer be seen a measurement is taken. This measurement is called the secchi disk depth. Another way to think of this is the visibility in the water.

Stop and think.

Who else, besides a trout, might be concerned about turbidity?

Below are instructions on how to make your own secchi disk.

Materials:

White plastic paint bucket lid with a small hole in the center to fit your eye-bolt

(below) Black permanent marker

Stainless steel eye-bolt, washer and nut of matching size

Depending on the depth of water you choose to measure - an appropriate length of cord that will fit through the eye-bolt

To weigh down the secchi disk, nuts and bolts to be placed evenly around the outer edge of the disk

Drill

Ruler

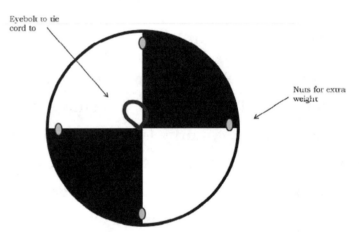

Directions:

1. Divide your bucket into 4 equal pieces (like a pie!)
2. Color 2 of the opposite "pieces" black
3. With the drill, drill 4 holes of the appropriate diameter (matching your smaller nuts and bolts) at 0°, 90°, 180°, and 270°
4. Place your nuts and bolts through these holes with the nuts on the underside (non- colored) of the disk
5. Assemble the eyebolt, washer and nut such that the eye of the bolt is on the black and white side of the disk and the washer and nut are on the opposing side.
6. Tie your cord to the eyebolt
7. Mark off measurements in the units of your choice using a ruler and permanent marker along the length of the cord starting at 0

CHAPTER FIVE

Extensions

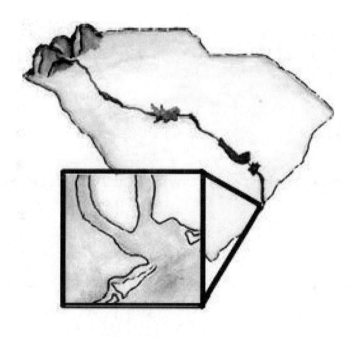

Making the Connection:

A Sticky Situation: Oil and Water

In Chapter 5, the characters arrived in a new ecosystem: a lake. They were immediately wisked away by an interesting character himself, Gary the Garfish. Gary showed them around and led them though their first hydroelectric dam.

After rushing through the dam Oscar and his friends made their way down the Saluda River. It was a big bummer when they noticed an oily slick on the surface of the water: pollution.

Pollution spoils things not just for animals but humans as well.

Take a moment to ponder the many ways pollution harms an ecosystem and its inhabitants.

There are many different sources and kinds of pollution. In this case oil has found its way into the river, most likely as stormwater runoff. Stormwater runoff is water from rain that has run typically over paved surfaces like roads and highways. It picks up substances like oil, and often ends up in rivers, lakes and streams.

While oil does not mix easily with water- it makes a HUGE mess. Often oil floats on the surface but oil spills can result in oily "tarballs" that eventually sink to pollute the riverbed or seafloor.

What are some ways we might clean-up oil spills?

The Environmental Protection Agency describes several ways we clean up, one of which is to soak it up with natural materials like ground corn cobs, hay – even feathers! To explore how tough it just might be let's experiment! This next activity needs some simple household items. Read on!

Activity: Clean it Up!

Materials:

Shallow bowl or plate

Water

Any type of oil from the pantry

Art materials, natural materials, disposable found objects in home/classroom

Feathers (from craft supply store)

Dish soap

Procedure (continued on the next page):

1. Add water to your plate

2. Sprinkle drops of oil over the top, to cover approximately half of the surface

3. Using various materials try to "clean up" your oil spill, including using feathers

4. Make observations and record in the space below:

What problems did you run into, if any?

Can you imagine this process going quickly? Taking a long time?

Was this hard? Easy?

Is this an effective way to clean up the oil?

What are other ideas or ways you could clean it up?

What about the feather? Is it dirty?

Imagine you are a bird with dirty, oily feathers.

Using the dish detergent, try to scrub your feather clean.

Did the feather come clean? Does the feather look the same?

Let it dry and see if it returns to its original shape and texture.

Looking further: Designing an Experiment

Scientists answer questions and design experiments using the scientific method. This is a way of thinking that helps to organize thoughts and the process of answering questions. It is often thought of as ending at the final conclusion (see chart below); however, usually experiments and the observations collected during them lead to more questions! Let's practice!

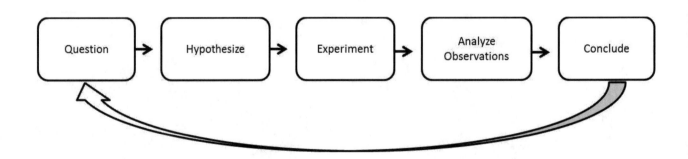

Step 1: Write your question here:

_____

_____

_____

_____

Step 2: Hypothesize: Brainstorm what the answer to your question might be:

_____

_____

_____

_____

Step 3: Design and carry out an experiment using the table below to get you started and a notebook. (See definitions of variables on the next page.) Remember, you must come up with a way to measure the changes in your dependent variable!

Independent Variable	Dependent Variable	Controlled Variables*

*hint: you will have more than 1

Independent variable: the "thing" in an experiment that you are manipulating or changing

Dependent variable: the variable that responds to the manipulation of the independent variable

Controlled variable: the "things" in the experiment that do not change- that are kept the same

Step 4: <u>Analyze your observations.</u> For example, if you measured the volume of oil each object removed several times (preforming what scientists called replications) you might take the mean volume removed for each object. Or, you might simply compare your volumes. **For example**:

feather		cotton		Paper towel
5 ml	>	4 ml	>	2 ml

Step 5: Draw a conclusion based on your analysis. In the example above, the feather

works best! What is your final conclusion?

_____

_____

_____

_____

_____

_____

**Ultimately, what are your feelings about this activity and what do you
think of pollution? Have your feelings stayed the same? Changed?**

CHAPTER SIX

Extensions

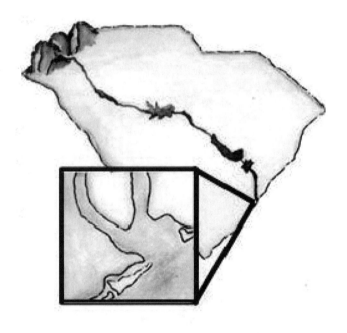

Making the Connection:

Lifting Fish

Boy! Oscar and his companions have been on quite some journey! So far they have traveled through a variety of South Carolina's regions and are finally about to make it into the coastal zone. Their last stop before exiting into Cooper River they meet Bob, a member of a very unigue striped bass population.

Bob's population of striped bass spends its entire life cycle in freshwater after being practically landlocked by dams. What is so special is the Bob belongs to a fish species that typically spends its whole life in saltwater returning only to freshwater where it was born to reproduce.

Nowadays, people who are in charge of the dams and others who are in charge of managing our natural resources have come up with a really cool way for other fish species like Bob and his friends to safely pass from Lake Moultrie to the Santee and Cooper Rivers: a fish elevator!

The elevator is in fact called the "fish lift", ushering fish safely between the different elevations of Lake Moultrie and the river systems below it.

Recall Oscar's journey through both the Dreher Shoals and Pinopolis Dams. They traveled with gravity from the lakes down into the turbines.

The St. Stephan's fish lift is open to the public. What makes it so neat is a viewing window that allows scientists and other onlookers to see the fish passing through the lift.

Why might scientists be interested in watching the fish pass through the lift? How would they make their observations?

Activity: One Fish, Two Fish

Scientists, as you may have guessed, like to make quantitative observations. These are observations with numbers. So, you guessed it! They COUNT the fish.

After they count the fish, they organize their information into tables. And the most important thing they might do with their table of fish species and numbers is to graph it! It is often much easier to see patterns and draw conclusions when you can see a picture of your numbers.

Below are some numbers based on real observations made by scientists in 2009*.

Fish Species	Number Passing Fish Lift
Striped Mullet	2,000
Freshwater Catfish	1,000
Striped Bass	175
Gizzard Shad	1,000
Longnose Gar	350
TOTAL:	**4,425**

*data can be found at www.dnr.sc.gov/fish/fishlift/chart2009.html

Using your knowledge of graphs, see if you can graph the numbers above.

Before you start, what kind of graph would work best?

Use the graph paper on the next page. Don't forget to label your axis!

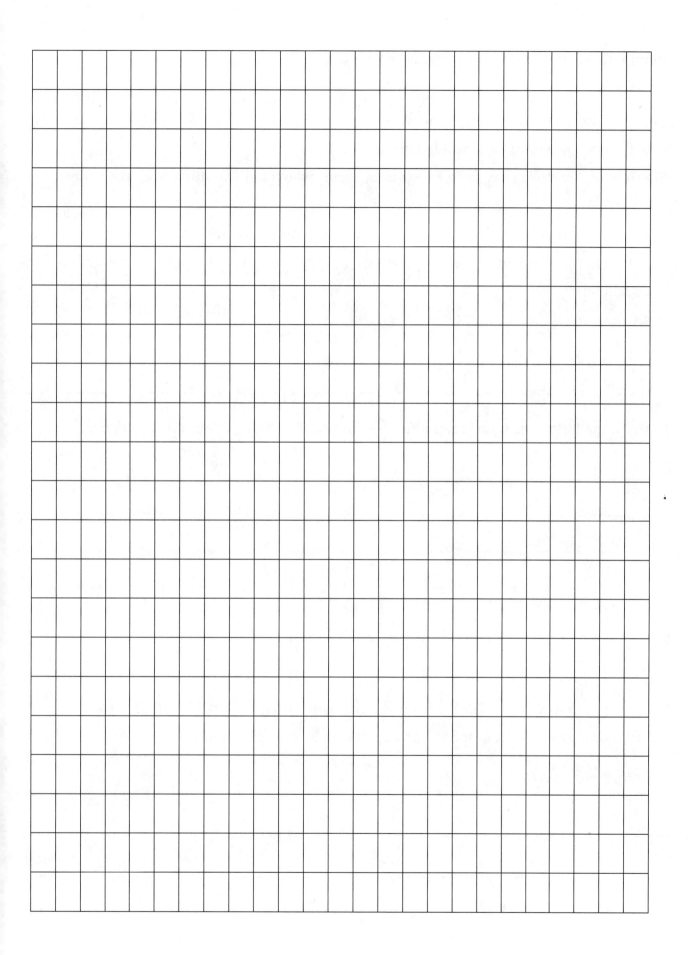

Answer the following questions about your graph:

1. What fish did scientists see the most of?

2. What fish did scientists see the least of?

3. Was there a big difference between the fish that was seen the most and seen the least?

4. Write a fraction to illustrate how many striped mullet passed through the lift out of the total number of fish (hint: use the table if you need to). Write your answer in the space below:

5. About how many fish is this out of the total number? $1/3$? $\frac{1}{4}$? $\frac{1}{2}$?

_____

6. On the lines below summarize the fishlift information with complete sentences:

_____

_____

_____

_____

_____

_____

7. Besides how many fish pass through the lift, what other information do these observations give you? (hint: look at the first column of the table).

_____

_____

_____

8. Why is this information important? (Think of an ecosystem and what it is made of.)

_____

_____

_____

_____

_____

_____

CHAPTER SEVEN

Extensions

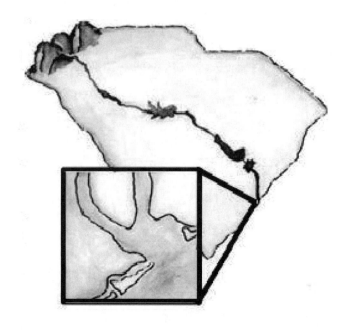

Making the Connection:

"Where the Rivers Meet the 'Sea', We Have an Estuary"

Well kids. It looks like they did it! Our crazy cast of characters has made it to the coastal zone, and almost to the ocean!

There is so much too see: from shorebirds to bridges, Charleston sure is one bustling port city! There is no shortage of things moving, coming and going - that is for sure. One of those things that is coming and going, would be the water Oscar and his friends are traveling in.

It doesn't take long for Oscar to bump into Nick and Clarence - the fellows that make up salt (their real names are sodium and chloride). Why would salt be in a river that is bringing freshwater to the coast?

Do you remember what you read in Chapter 7? What explanation did Nick and Clarence give?

You got it! Tides! Tides are caused by gravity. Gravity is a natural force that pulls large planetary bodies towards one another. The moon and the sun both pull on Earth's water. Because the moon is much closer to the Earth than the sun, it is normally what we talk about most when we discuss tides. We see tides as a change in water level. On a "high tide" salty ocean water enters estuaries and rivers close to the coast. On a "low tide" that salty ocean water recedes back into the ocean.

Hey! While we are talking about salt water- let's think about solutions!

In a saltwater solution, what is the

1.   solute? _____
2.   solvent? _____

Let's recall the idea of a solution's concentration. That would be how much solute is dissolved in your solvent.

How might a change in tide affect the concentration of salt in the water of an estuary like Charleston Harbor?

Do you think changes in water level and in salinity affect the biotic components of an estuary?

How might chnages in water level affect people? Activity: Tracking Tides

Tides are important to recreational boaters, commercial fisherman and container ship captains- just to name a few. In February of 2012, the Ports Authority had BIG job to do. It had to move massive cranes, hundreds of feet tall, underneath the Arthur Ravenel Bridge to get them to a new location upstream. Even after taking the cranes apart they were still too tall to safely get the job done. The only choice left: to let Mother Nature handle the rest.

It was decided that the cranes would be moved at low tide. **Tidal data is often shown as a line graph. Let's graph the tides from that week in 2012 when the cranes were moved.**

You will need to create your x and y axis, and use the 2 columns of the table below as your x and y coordinates. What might you label your x axis? Your y axis?

(x) **Time of Day**	(y) **Height of water*** (feet)
2:00am	-0.5
8:00am	5.5
2:30pm	-0.5
8:30pm	5.5

*data rounded, obtained from NOAA; tidal predictions for Feb. 22, 2012; height of water relative to MLLW

Graph:

Answer the following questions about your graph:

1. By just glancing at the graph, can you easily tell what tides are low and what tides are high? _____

2. If the people in charge of moving the cranes safely decided that the crane could only pass under the bridge if the water level was 1.5 feet or lower, what time of day must the crane be moved? _____

3. How long does it have to move, keeping question 2 in mind? _____

CHAPTER EIGHT

Extensions

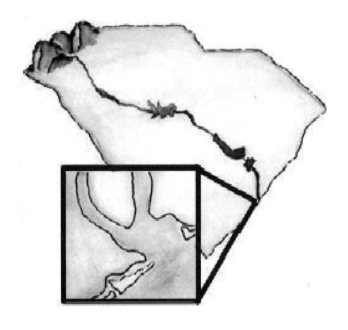

Making the Connection

Don't Forget the Small Guy! Silly cells...

While life is all around us - and all around Oscar, Hank and Hannah - don't forget the SMALLEST unit of life, the cell. Pretty sure Oscar and his buddies won't forget.

After admiring the beautiful estuary and all of the forms of life it holds, Oscar and his friends entered a plant-like planktonic cell – a diatom! A plant-like what??

Plankton are the drifters of the ocean. Whether they are large or small plankton are pushed around by currents, wind and waves. They are unable to swim against these forces. Examples of plankton include diatoms, such as the one you read about in Chapter 8, and even jellyfish! The opposite of plankton are nekton. Nekton are organisms that can propel themselves in a particular direction, like fish.

Plankton can be divided into plant-like plankton and animal-like plankton. Plant-like plankton are much like plants that live on land. They both use energy from the sun to produce their own food. Producers are extremely important as they are the foundation of food chains on land and in water. The diatom that Oscar, Hank and Hannah ran into is one of those important producers. The cool thing is- it is made of just ONE cell!

Cells are the smallest unit of life. Even though they are the smallest units of life, they are made up of tiny parts too! Each tiny part, whether it is a membrane or what is called an organelle, preforms an important job.

Do a bit of research on plant and animal cells. Can you define:

cell membrane –

cytoplasm –

nucleus –

vacuole –

Activity: Make a cell!

Materials:

Jello

Pie tin (for a round cell) or cake pan (square cell)

Art supplies or for an entirely edible cell use fruit

Procedure:

1. Pick a plant or animal cell- even make a model diatom just like in the story if you want!

2. Using art materials or food, make up the cell structures you researched and place them in either your pan or pie tin.

3. Follow the instructions on the back of the jello packet and pour over your newly made cell structures! Wait until set and voila! You have your own SILLY CELL!

Oscar and Operation Oil Spill

The air was heavy and wet with humidity. It was the kind that sticks to a person's skin. Even at this early hour, Oscar the oxygen atom noticed the uncomfortable weather. Oscar had hoped that, after having been in Charleston for a while, he would have been used to it by now. But that just wasn't the case. It was not quite nine o'clock in the morning, and already he was dreading just how hot the day was forecasted to get.

Oscar was relaxing in the Ashley River with Hank and Hannah. They were riding the tide down towards Charleston Harbor and very much trying to cool off. Some swirling water had them caught by a piling where Oscar's friend Dorothy the Pelican was resting. It was a nice piling by all accounts, and it gave Dorothy a wonderful view of the river. Oscar wondered what the brilliant green of the salt marsh might look like from up there.

Oscar also wondered what appeared to be up with Dorothy. Dorothy is normally quite calm and friendly, but this morning her feathers were definitely ruffled. She was acting strangely.

"Hey Dorothy", Oscar called up to her. "What has got you looking upset?"

Dorothy cocked her head to the side to get a better view of her friend. With one eye she peered down at Oscar. The look on her face was stern and troubled as the breeze blew the tiny feathers on her face into a frown.

Dorothy sighed, "It seems we have an emergency just down the way, Oscar. Earlier this morning, the Coast Guard boats zoomed towards a vessel near Fort Sumter. It was," Dorothy started to stammer, "it was, uh, ummm, it was suspected of leaking OIL!"

"Oh no!" exclaimed Oscar. "Well, what is being done? Is it bad? Dorothy, please tell me it isn't very bad!" Hank and Hannah's eyes were wide with fear, but they stayed quiet, hoping Dorothy would provide some good news.

Dorothy fluffed her feathers and shook her head and body, as if she could fluff the stickiness of the situation away. "Oscar, the first responders and scientists are out in full force. Look, the humans didn't mean to pollute the harbor, and at least they are working to fix the problem. They will find the person responsible and hold them accountable!"

Really, it didn't seem very convincing, and it appeared Dorothy was just trying to convince herself that it would be fine.

"Dorothy, thanks for the information. This is something I have to check out for myself. Which way should we go?" asked Oscar.

"Well, dear, there is only one way to go. That would be with the tide. I am not sure where all of the hustle and bustle is at the moment. Let's just hope that it all turns out okay."

"Thanks, Dorothy; I guess we should try to get going now." And with that, Oscar let the swirling water carry him away from the piling and his wise friend.

The tide sure was moving and it had Oscar's mind racing. *OIL SPILL*! Those were about the worst words he could have imagined hearing. Sure, he had heard of them and all of the damage they could cause. In all honesty, Oscar was a bit surprised. Considering all he had been through on planet Earth, he had never seen a large spill. Oscar remembered a time during his last adventure. He and his friends had seen a small oily slick and insects trapped and struggling in the shiny substance. He had heard that experts say there are tens of thousands reported oil spills each year in the United States alone. He had also heard how oil spills harm ecosystems and both the living and nonliving factors that make them up.

Oil is a sticky, toxic substance that can cover everything in its path. It can harm and kill wildlife by accidentally being consumed or even inhaled. From birds to oysters to turtles to humans - no one benefits from an oil spill. And the worst part is that oil is very hard to clean up. Oscar shook his head. *This is just too bad*, he thought. Not in his beautiful coastal ecosystem!

But maybe, just maybe the humans can fix it. And maybe scientists are learning about new ways to help the animals and plants that are affected! And maybe engineers are working on ways to keep oil spills from happening! Oscar was having a hard time seeing the good in an oil spill, but was trying to remain positive. Maybe he would get there, and it wouldn't be so bad.

As if someone read his mind Oscar suddenly heard a loud mechanical whirring overhead. A bright orange Coast Guard helicopter was circling this section of the river. "I wonder how this helps out," Oscar said out loud to himself.

"Well, actually, it is one of the very first things responders do. They try to track the oil and map where it is and where it is going," said a voice out of the blue.

Oscar jumped. "Sheesh! I had no idea we were next to anybody," Oscar exclaimed. "You scared me!"

"You are *always* next to someone out here," replied Oscar's good friend, Tiny the Diamondback Terrapin.

"Well, boy oh boy, Tiny, it is good to see you! All of this commotion has got me very worked up," said Oscar. "It also has Hank and Hannah stunned into silence."

Their two sad faces nodded in agreement.

"You aren't the only one worked up. The humans are running around everywhere. From the first responders to the scientists and everyone investigating the leaked oil, there are many tasks to be done," Tiny explained, "All of us terrapins are alarmed, without a doubt. You see, we lay our eggs in the safety of the marsh and hibernate in the marsh during the winter..."

Oscar interrupted, "Wait a minute. The spill is in the MARSH?!"

"Unfortunately, Oscar, the spill is in the water and where the water goes, the oil goes, too."

"Just the same as me, I guess," replied Oscar gloomily. The tide was pushing him along and away from his friend. "It was good to see you, Tiny!" Oscar waved goodbye limply, as Tiny's distraught face grew harder and harder to see.

Boy! This surely was a mess. And all of Oscar's friends were equally upset. Oscar's eyes were drawn to the horizon as buildings and bridges came into view. He was coming up quickly on a marina. A marina is much like a parking lot for boats, but in the water, and this marina was very busy. Humans were all around. Some of them appeared to be the boat owners. Shielding their eyes from the sun, Oscar saw many arms outstretched, pointing at the boats and at the water. Some voices sounded frustrated and angry. Other voices were trying to provide answers and calm people down. Another eddy swirled Oscar close to a dock where he was able to observe all of the action. *Goodness*, thought Oscar. *The spill is in the marina! Oil can't be good for people's property either.*

Oscar suddenly noticed several individuals that stood out from the crowd. They had all sorts of equipment with them, like walkie-talkies and clipboards. They were walking closer, and Oscar listened in as they spoke to one another. They were scientists!

"Alright, Sean and Sarah," said a tall slender man with glasses. "This is a good opportunity to take a bad situation and learn from it. We are going to set up an experiment to figure out how marsh grass is affected by this oil. Do you think you all can handle that?" The man was making all sorts of motions with his arms and pointing to a flooded area of marsh, where a lot of oil had come to rest. The two young scientists nodded, took the equipment and got started. Oscar thought this was so interesting. Despite the spill, he couldn't wait to find out more about what the scientists were doing!

As Oscar continued to watch the scientists, he noticed a young man that looked like some sort of official walking with a marina employee. He appeared to be counting something and making notes in a journal. Oscar soon discovered the man was trying to estimate the amount of oil that was trapped in the marina. "It's just like Tiny said. The humans want to know how much oil there is, where it is, and what it will do to our ecosystem!" Oscar muttered to himself in amazement.

The tide suddenly whisked them away and Oscar, Hank and Hannah drifted under bridges to find themselves in Charleston Harbor. The oil was still all around the trio. With the helicopters buzzing overhead, Oscar tried to think positively. "Don't worry Hank. Don't worry Hannah. This will all get figured out. We have to trust the humans."

Humans can accidentally cause harm to the planet, but they sure do make up for it when they try to resolve their problems. The scientists, surveyors and first responders all gave Oscar hope that he would hear very soon that the oil had been cleaned up and the people that caused the spill would be found.

Extensions

1. Oscar, Hank and Hannah came across a person who was working on figuring out how much oil was in the marina. Information about how much oil there is can be important for many reasons. For example, it could help determine the amount of a fine for the people at fault, and it could also help determine how much money could be given to the boat owners and marina for any damages. Help our surveyor figure out how much oil has spilled into these 4 rectangular boat slips (a slip is like a parking spot, but for a boat!):

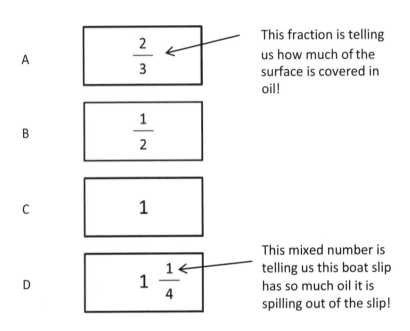

A $\frac{2}{3}$ — This fraction is telling us how much of the surface is covered in oil!

B $\frac{1}{2}$

C 1

D $1\frac{1}{4}$ — This mixed number is telling us this boat slip has so much oil it is spilling out of the slip!

1A) (*Standards 5.NSF.1, 5.NSF.2*)

The surveyor wants to know how much of the 4 boats slips' surfaces are covered in oil. What might we need to do? Using your knowledge of fractions, add the numbers from boat slips A, B, C and D. Don't forget to use a common denominator! Show your work and turn your final answer into a mixed number.

Complete this sentence with your final answer:

_____ out of a total of 4 boat slips have their surfaces covered in oil.

1B) (*Standards 4.MDA.3, 5.NSF.3 ,5.NSF.5*)

Using the length (10 ft.) and width (4 ft.) of the boat slips, calculate the area in feet that is covered in oil for boat slips B, C, and D. We will use boat slip A in an example below:

10 feet

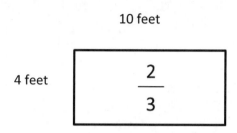

4 feet

Example: 4 feet x 10 feet = 40 feet²

$$40 \text{ feet}^2 \quad \times \quad \frac{2}{3} \quad = \quad \frac{80}{3} \text{ feet}^2$$

You can turn your final answer from an improper fraction into a mixed number:

$$\frac{80}{3} \text{ feet}^2 \quad = \quad 26 \frac{2}{3} \text{ feet}^2$$

Now complete the same for B, C, and D using the space below to show your work:

1C) (*Standards 5.MDA.1, 5.MDA.3, 5.NSF.4A*)

Great job so far! Now we are going to practice calculating volume. It turns out that the oil isn't just floating on the surface, but is also **6 inches deep**. Do you remember the formula for volume of a rectangular prism? Good! Using the image below to help you, calculate the volume of oil that could be in **boat slip B**!

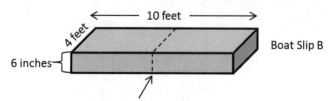

* Remember that it appears that Boat Slip B is half covered in oil. Use the dashed line to help you imagine this.

1D) (*Standards 5.MDA.4*)

Describe the difference between area and volume in the space below:

2. (*Standards: Math: 5.G.1, 5.G.2, Science: 5.S.1A.4, 5.S.1A.5, 5.S.1A.6, 5.S.1A.7, 5.S.1A.8, 5.E.3B*)

Oscar and his friends also saw some scientists working on an experiment during their time at the marina. Oscar found a copy of their notes. Using their notes on the next page, help Oscar determine what the results of the experiment were by using the information in the table to create a **line graph on the chart below. Create a title and label your x and y axis. Use the graph as evidence to argue for or against the scientists' hypothesis.**

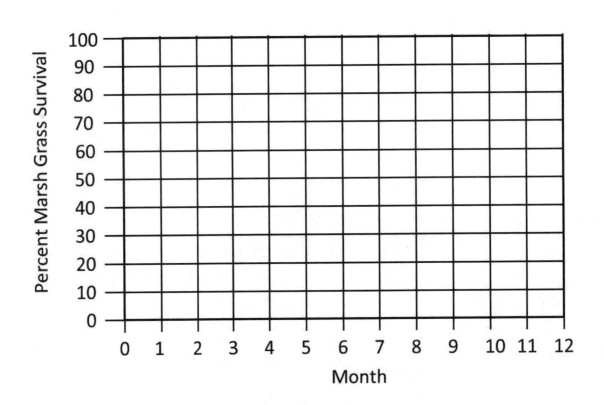

Note to teachers:
The data is loosely based on information found in the following NOAA document:

http://response.restoration.noaa.gov/sites/default/files/Oil_Spills_in_Marshes.pdf)

Notes

Question:
How will oil affect the survival recovery of the salt marsh grass?

Hypothesis:
We think that oil will kill the marsh grass and that it will take more than 1 year to recover.

(x   ,   y)

Month	Marsh Grass Survival (in percent)
0	
1	100
2	50
3	40
4	30
5	20
6	20
7	20
8	30
9	30
10	40
11	40
12	40
	40

Alright folks, I know what you are thinking. The title of this little ditty I am starring in sounds pretty impressive. And, believe me, it is. Right about now, you might be imagining me in a flowing cape, spear in hand, riding in on my stallion with throngs of soldiers at my side. Or, hey, I could have bulging biceps the size of small watermelons, standing with my hands poised on my hips and perched atop a tall mountain with my head in the clouds, looking out across my kingdom.

Don't get me wrong, that'd be awesome. But what happened to me just the other day was equally cool in my book. And, it was quite an adventure. I promise.

You might also be wondering how my book project is going. You know. I am working on chronicling all of my journeys. I mean, after all, I have so much to share. What's that? You didn't know? Hmmph. Well now you do. And without further delay, now you can check out the story of this great invasion…

 **The South Carolina Lowcountry** truly is a sight to behold. Bright greens, rich blues and deep browns are transported from your sense of sight suddenly to your nose by a gentle breeze carrying a whiff of pluff mud. Distant calls of seabirds and symphonies of crickets and cicadas add another dimension to the already overwhelming experience. It really is a place I never want to leave. Plus, the seafood is good. (Hey, I love shrimp. What can I say?)

I was hanging out with Hank and Hannah (what's new) in one of my favorite spots in Charleston Harbor, a mudflat on the southwest side. We had a fabulous view of the Arthur Ravenel Bridge with the USS *Yorktown* in the distance. To my right was the historical Fort Sumter. In fact, the tract of land just up behind the mudflat we were lounging on also had historical importance. It had been the site of Fort Johnson, from which the Confederates fired the first shots on Fort Sumter, starting the Civil War. The main reason I enjoyed this spot, however, was because of the scientists. I had had run-ins and overheard facts and numbers, seen experiments from a distance, but boy oh boy I had never been inside a real laboratory. This area on James Island was home to many scientists and their research buildings. Behind me, stood the building for the Marine Resources Division of the South Carolina Department of Natural Resources, and down the way were more scientists from different organizations. I even heard there were students out here! Wow, I wish I could study with them.

I was suddenly jolted out of my research-laden daydream, when a dark shadow appeared over our heads, blocking out the sun. The shadow was getting larger and larger, threatening to press down upon us. It was no longer just a shadow. It was a BOOT! We were going to get squished! Stepped on! Flattened!

"AAAAAAAAHHHHHHHHHHHHHH!" we all shrieked in unison.

"This is it!" screamed Hank.

"Someone save us!" cried Hannah.

And then, (thank goodness) there was what seemed like an eternity as the boot was suspended above our heads, just inches away from pummeling us deep into the mud.

Suddenly, it jerked awkwardly to the left, then to the right.

"Oh no," groaned Hannah. "The human attached to that boot is falling! Look out!!"

I had broken out into a cold sweat. Hank seemed completely frozen with a look of terror on his face. Hannah was shaking like a leaf and shouting inaudibly. The human was wobbling, faltering, and began to topple as if in a bad slow motion horror film. Instinctively, we ducked. There was nowhere to run. And just as soon as we were sure we were goners, the young lady attached to the boot was grabbed and steadied by her friend. Her boot came down with a thud next to us as we breathed a sigh of relief.

Apparently the humans thought it was the best thing ever and laughed hysterically.

"There is nothing funny about this," said Hannah angrily.

"Well, they sure think there is," retorted Hank.

In truth the humans were howling like a pack of hyenas and holding their sides, as their fit of laughter had them practically doubled over. All of that laughter was a bit infectious, and I began to laugh myself. What started out as a quiet chuckle erupted in a loud guffaw. Hank and Hannah looked absolutely puzzled, but they caught the bug and started laughing, too.

No sooner had we laughed ourselves silly, than the ground started to shake underneath us. In the blink of an eye, we had been scooped up and placed in some sort of container. Oh brother. We had been so caught up in our laughing that we hadn't noticed what the two human friends were doing. We didn't need to wait long for an answer. It seemed the mud we had been lounging on literally came to life! All of a sudden there was so much chatter I just couldn't keep it straight!

"The scientists have us!"

"This will be fun!"

"This is terrifying!"

"Am I in an... an experiment?"

There was yelling and shouting and all sorts of ideas. Then a voice shouted above the rest: "Quiet!" And quiet it became. "My name is Annie. Some call me Annie the Amphipod."

At this moment, I wondered what on earth an amphipod was, but there seemed to be quite a few of them along for the ride. Truthfully, they looked a lot like tiny shrimp. Annie cleared her throat and began to speak again. "I have been through this before, and it will all turn out just fine. These scientists here are conducting some very important research on that... that... *thing* that is in here with all of us."

"Huh? What *thing* are you talking about?" I chimed in.

"You mean to tell me you didn't happen to notice what you are sitting on?" Annie replied.

I looked around only to realize we were all tangled in a giant mass of what looked like brown spaghetti. It filled up our tiny cramped space, sticking to it and dangling from the lid.

"Oh my! Will it hurt us?" I asked.

"Well, it won't hurt us directly, but that is what the scientists are trying to find out. They want to know more about this *thing* and how it affects our ecosystems. It is an INVADER!" Annie explained.

"Well, can we please stop calling it a *thing*," said a voice from behind me. I turned to see a worm hanging out of his tube-shaped home. "It is a type of seaweed and is biotic just like all of us are. That means living, for those of you who don't know. It is living and producing its own energy every day, using the sun."

"You mean it uses photosynthesis?" piped a tiny hermit crab.

"Yes. Yes indeed. It also happens to be an invasive species, as Ms. Annie mentioned. That means it isn't originally from this area but now calls this ecosystem home." said the tubeworm.

At this point, I was simply amazed at how much everyone with us knew about the place they lived in and the living factors that lived amongst them. I guess I shouldn't have been surprised. After all, they did live near a bunch of scientists.

Satisfied with my reasoning, I inquired, "Mr. Worm, how do you know all of this?"

"Because, my new friend, I collect the seaweed. As it floats past, I grab it and secure it to my tube. I really do know it quite well."

I wanted to ask more questions, but it seemed that was not going to happen, as the two researchers opened the container to remove the contents. Hank, Hannah and I ended up with the invasive seaweed on a cold black counter top. Well, if we were fairly safe, and I wasn't to be too concerned, I might as well try to learn something.

I looked around the fluorescently lit room and saw shelves upon shelves of supplies. There were computers and cabinets and all sorts of machines buzzing and whirring. There were tubes and trays scattered about. And there was also a lot of friendly chatter. The researchers were very excited as they poured over there work. A sign on the door said *Dr. Erik Sotka*. He must be the scientist that is in charge.

No sooner did I see the sign, than Dr. Sotka turned the corner. He waved in a friendly manner to his team of scientists and motioned them over to a big desk. They were going to have a meeting! This was great!

"We will get to learn so much", I said to Hank and Hannah excitedly.

They seemed to be as interested as I was. We leaned in closer, eyes wide with curiosity…

Continue your journey (with a grown-up!) online at:
www.patriotspointsciencespotlight.com.

Learn what Oscar, Hank and Hannah learned, and become a part of the scientific process by helping Dr. Sotka and his team with REAL RESEARCH! Oscar can't wait to see you there!

Writing
Exercises

Pick one of the following topics to write several explanatory paragraphs about. Introduce your topic clearly and include at least two definitions and two facts. Include a picture if you would like.

A) invasive plants in South Carolina lakes

B) the food chain in an estuary

C) how people use water to make electricity

_____

_____

_____

_____

_____

_____

_____

_____

_____

_____

Consider re-telling how and when Gus became deposited from Gus's point of view. Using this alternative view write a short narrative and include dialogue, descriptive details and imagery.

_____

_____

_____

_____

_____

_____

_____

_____

_____

_____

Write an argument to support the idea that matter is neither created nor destroyed, but instead recycled. Use information from different resources as evidence. Connect your claims to Oscar, Hank and Hannah's journey.

_____

_____

_____

_____

_____

_____

_____

_____

_____

_____